DATE DUE

▬1 JUN '88	
JUN 3 '88 *Ret'd*	
UPI SPO-125	PRINTED IN U.S.A.

LIBYA
SINCE THE REVOLUTION

LIBYA
SINCE THE REVOLUTION

Aspects of Social
and Political Development

Marius K. Deeb
and Mary Jane Deeb

PRAEGER SPECIAL STUDIES • PRAEGER SCIENTIFIC

Library of Congress Cataloging in Publication Data

Deeb, Marius.
　　Libya since the revolution.

　　Bibliography: p.
　　Includes index.
　　1. Libya—Social conditions.　2. Libya—Politics and
government—1969-　　　 I. Deeb, Mary Jane.　II. Title.
HN785.A8D4　　　　　961'.2　　　　　81-19985
ISBN 0-03-058308-X　　　　　　　　　　AACR2

Published in 1982 by Praeger Publishers
CBS Educational and Professional Publishing
a Division of CBS Inc.
521 Fifth Avenue, New York, New York 10175 U.S.A.

© 1982 by Praeger Publishers

23456789　145　987654321

Printed in the United States of America

CONTENTS

LIST OF TABLES

INTRODUCTION

This book studies Libya's social and political development since the 1969 Revolution and the problems this society has faced when it has attempted to introduce changes in its socioeconomic structure and modernize its institutions.

We have chosen to deal with the aspects which have undergone the greatest change since the revolution and yet have received the least attention in scholarly works on modern Libya. The discovery of oil and the economic boom which followed has been studied, to some extent, in works on the Libyan economy, as has been the rise of al-Qadhdhafi to political power in the last decade. However, the impact of the historical coincidence of the oil boom, with the rise of a revolutionary regime in Libya a few years later, on the internal structure of the society as well as on its ideology, has not been covered. It is that gap which we have tried to fill in this work, by going in depth into the various aspects of the structure, institutions, ideology and foreign policy of Libya, and analyzing the changes that occurred spontaneously, and those that were introduced as a matter of policy by the state. In each chapter we have attempted to point to the dialectical process taking place between traditional structures, institutions, and values, and those being superimposed by a socialist government, Western technology, and the social and political upheavals in the region.

By opening the book with a chapter on the problems of urbanization in Tripoli, we are in a sense starting from the general problem of a fast developing third world country that has found itself almost overnight transformed from one of the poorest countries in the world to one of the richest. It is the least specifically Libyan aspect of development, as the problems faced by the city of Tripoli are those faced by the capitals of many other developing countries in Africa and Asia. The difference in Libya's case is that unlike most developing countries, Libya has the economic capacity to handle those problems. Consequently the issue here is one of planning for alternative ways of diverting the flow of population from one or two major urban centers to other regions of the country in order to prevent lopsided development. The need to build new cities to accommodate the rapid natural increase of the population, the rising expectations of the youth, the large foreign work force, and the creation of new industries, may be one of the single most powerful forces that will change the social structure of the country in the decades to come. The shift in population, the creation of new institutions, the building of cities to which no one group, tribe, clan, or ethnic minority has any claim upon, and the physical environment of Western buildings, will all have a tremendous impact on the values, world views, and mental structures of the generation that is now still in primary school.

Education, the second aspect of development with which we deal in this book, is again one shared with most developing countries in the world. Its cultural specificity lies in its chequered historical growth, the various influences that have shaped it, and the forces that at times halted its natural course and at other times diverted it into specific channels. Hence the importance of the historical background of the chapter on education, which the authors prepared in order to give the reader a more meaningful picture of the educational system in Libya today and the problems it faces.

Of the three chapters on the social aspects of development in Libya it is the one on women that is the most specific to that society. Women in this chapter have been placed in their cultural context with a background of the traditional social, religious, legal, and regional forces that have molded their roles and identities for a great many centuries. It would be impossible even to begin to comprehend the tremendous upheaval that is taking place today in the Libyan society in relation to the role of women, without first gaining insight into those forces of tradition that have woven so intricately, and for so long, the social fabric of the Libyan society. Changing, for a woman in Libya, means breaking away from those traditions that gave her, since birth, security and a stable place within the structure of her family and tribe. It means entering a new and unfamiliar world where none of the women of her family can guide her. It means carrying the burden of generations of taboos and social constraints that have crippled women's initiatives, searching for a personal identity, and trying to shed some of the fears attached to them. And yet, inexorably, change is taking place, with old concepts of women's roles slowly eroding, and being replaced by new ones, more appropriate to a rapidly changing society.

In the fourth chapter we deal with the relationship between Islam and politics in Libya, an aspect of development fundamental to the understanding of the policies of most countries in the Middle East. But whereas Islamic fundamentalism shows signs of revival in Iran, Turkey, and Egypt, for instance, the de facto secularism and separation between religious matters and mundane matters are gaining ascendancy. The specific nature of this relationship in revolutionary Libya is rooted in the religious movement of the Sanusiya. Al-Qadhdhafi was tremendously influenced by the Sanusiya legacy that he tried to transcend, and in so doing, transformed the role of Islam in Libya, a transformation that occurred also as a result of his hostile encounter with men of religion and jurists over political and social issues. Their opposition to his radical ideology forced him to curb their power by advocating and practicing a de facto secularism.

The fifth chapter, dealing with the social basis of the revolution, puts al-Qadhdhafi's revolutionary conception of Islam in the wider context of the social origins of his ideology and its implications. In this chapter we have also given a brief apperçu of Libya's fragmented and segmented socioeconomic social structure on the eve of the revolution, and of the predominant role of the non-Libyans in the economy. We have attempted to relate the basic features of the socioeconomic structure to the origins of al-Qadhdhafi's social and economic ideology. The latter has not been treated as a mere ideology but rather as a guide for policies that were put into effect during the 1970s, and that transformed the relationship between different sectors of the society: employers and workers, landlords and tenants, producers and consumers. The changes that took place in the society during the last decade are seen here not only in the light of al-Qadhdhafi's policies, but also as rooted in his own personal vision of a precapitalist 'ideal' society, a view affected by his own tribal and petit bourgeois experience in Syrtica, Sabha, and Misrata.

The sixth and final chapter of this book deals with Libya's Arab policy since 1969. It examines the development in stages of that policy, taking the most pertinent political issues, such as the Arab-Israeli conflict, the bid for regional leadership, support of liberation and revolutionary movements, and Arab unity, as the foci for analysis. The activity Arab policy of revolutionary Libya is in direct contrast to the relatively isolationist and to some degree parochial policies of the Sanusi monarchy that preceded it. Al-Qadhdhafi's continuous drive to enhance Libya's stature politically and change its role from a minor Arab force to that of a major actor on the regional scene of Arab politics, has been examined here in some detail. We have also pointed out the special relationship between Egypt and Libya, and the basic impact the former power has had directly or indirectly on Libya in general and on its Arab foreign policy in particular.

In this manner we have covered the major aspects of development in Libya since its revolution. Each aspect would not be complete without an understanding of the others: hence the emancipation of women, for instance, could not take place without a change in the education system; al-Qadhdhafi's concept of the role of Islam could not be fully explained without an understanding of the social history and the social forces within the Libyan society; and Libya's somewhat erratic Arab foreign policy cannot be understood in a vacuum but must be related to al-Qadhdhafi's social and political ideology.

LIBYA
SINCE THE REVOLUTION

Chapter 1

A DEMOGRAPHIC PROFILE OF GREATER TRIPOLI

INTRODUCTION

The purpose of this chapter is twofold. First, it will give a picture of the muhafadha (province) of Greater Tripoli in terms of rate of increase and growth (birthrate, deathrate, and migration) as well as describe the type of population in terms of the predominant characteristics: urban, rural, age, and sex. Second, the implications of these demographic characteristics that are affecting the processes of urbanization and development of Tripoli will be analyzed.

ADMINISTRATIVE DIVISIONS OF GREATER TRIPOLI

Greater Tripoli is divided administratively into six municipalities: al-Qarbulli, Tajura, the municipality of Tripoli, Janzur, Qasr bin Ghashir, and al-'Aziziya (see Table 1.1). Tripoli, Qasr bin Ghashir, and al-'Aziziya are further subdivided into fir' baladiya, or sectors: Tripoli has five such sectors, Qasr bin Ghashir has four, and al-'Aziziya has two. Each municipality and each fir' baladiya is in turn broken down into smaller units called mahallas.[1] (See Table 1.2.) The interesting point to note here is that the mahallas are administrative divisions that are based primarily on existing social and spatial divisions. A large number of mahallas are named after one of the tribes which traditionally occupied that particular area.[2] Some members of those qaba'il or tribes still live in their areas today, although most of the younger generations have moved out to more "modern" or fashionable areas.[3] Thus the administrative unit of the mahalla is just an official recognition of the existing divisions

1

TABLE 1.1

Administrative Divisions of Greater Tripoli
(showing municipalities and their sectors)

Municipalities	Sectors or Fir' Baladiya
Al-Qarbulli	Al-Qarbulli
Tajura	Tajura
Tripoli	Tripoli
	Al-Hadba
	Qarqarish
	Suq al-Jum'a
	Al-Furnaj
Janzur	Janzur
Qasr bin Ghashir	Qasr bin Ghashir
	Sidi al-Sa'ih
	Suq al-Khamis
	'Usbi'a
Al-'Aziziya	Al-'Aziziya
	Al-Suwani

Source: Based on information gathered from LAR,
Ministry of Planning, Census and Statistics Department,
Al-Dalil al-Jughrafi, Muhafadha' Tarablus (Tripoli:
al-Matba'a al-Libiya, 1973).

within the city. However, not all municipalities in Greater Tripoli
have a traditional set of qaba' il who inhabit them, some areas being
exclusively commercial areas and others being settled by foreign or
by rural-migrant groups. Qarqarish, for instance, is an area with
no traditional ties. Built originally by the Italians, they kept it exclusively for themselves, preventing Libyan families from living there.
Although this has changed since World War II, Qarqarish has remained a largely foreign quarter, with high-rent housing, modern
department stores, supermarkets, and first-class hotels all catering,
at least in part, to the foreign communities.

MAIN URBAN CENTERS IN GREATER TRIPOLI

Tripoli city (the municipality) is the main urban center in the
muhafadha. It has four major suburbs at radial distances of 20 to 25
kilometers from the center of the city itself. Those were originally

TABLE 1.2

The Mahallas of Greater Tripoli

Municipality	Mahalla	Municipality	Mahalla
Al-Qarbulli	Al-Karawa	Tripoli	Suq al-Jum'a
	Al-Sharqiya	(continued)	sector
	Al-Ruwaj		Al-Nasr
	Al-'Ataya		'Aqba bin-Nafi'
	Al-Qawi'a		Al-Jala'
	Al-Khawaliq		Al-Harat
			'Arada
Tripoli	Tripoli sector		'Amr bin al-'As
	Bab al-Bahr		Sidi al-Marghani
	Humat al-baladiya		Al-Gharbiya
	Abi al-Khayr		Al-Sahil
	Kushat al-Sifar		
	Humat Gharyan		Al-Furnaj sector
	Mizran		Quz Zanata
	Al-Dhahra		Jami' 'Ar'ara
	Ziwayat al-		'Ayn Zara
	Dahmani		Al-Hashan
	Shari' al-Shat		Al-Fath
	Fashlum		Sidi Abu Gharara
	Al-Manshiya		
	Al-Nuflin	Janzur	Al-Sharqiya
			Al-Suq
	Al-Hadba sector		Sidi 'Abd al-Latif
	Bab 'Akara		Al-Wast
	Bab bin Ghashir		Sayyad
	Sidi Salim		Al-'Aqab
	Shari' al-Zawiya		
	Shari' al-Bayk	Qasr bin	Qasr bin Ghashir
	Abu Harida	Ghashir	sector
	Shari' al-Sarim		Suq al-Sabt
	Al-Hay al-Andalus		Al-Matar
			Al-'Awanin
	Qarqarish sector		Bi'r al-Tuta
	Qarqarish		Khuwaylid
	Al-Shari' al-		Rudud al-Zawiya
	Gharbi		
	Ghut al-Shu'al		Sidi al-Sa'ih sector
			Sidi al-Sa'ih
			Al-Ghalaya
			Abu 'Aisha

(continued)

TABLE 1.2, continued

Municipality	Mahalla	Municipality	Mahalla
Qasr bin Ghashir (continued)	Sidi al-Sa'ih sector (continued) Al-Tuba Bi'r Dhiyab Suq al-Khamis sector Sidi al-Jilani Amsihil Bil-rish Sidi-Jabir Usbi'a sector Awlad Abu 'A'isha Awlad Ahmad Bani'Ataya Sidi Abu 'Arqub Awlad Murghim	Al-'Aziziya (continued)	Al-'Aziziya sector (continued) Bi'r al-Jadid Al-Sa'adiya Al-'Amariya Al-Suwani sector Al-Suwani Al-Najila Jami' al-Tughar
Al-'Aziziya	Al-'Aziziya sector Wadi al-Hira Al-Sharqiya Al-Gharbiya	Tajura	Al-Wadi al-Gharbi Al-Wadi al-Sharqi Abi al-Ashhar Al-Burhaniya Al-Hamidiya Al-Mashay Al-'Uthmaniya

Source: LAR, Ministry of Planning, Census and Statistics Department, Al Dalil al-Juphuaji, Muhafadhat Tarablus (Tripoli: Al-Matba'a al-Libiya, 1973), pp. 89-104.

rural areas that became part of the city as it expanded in all directions. Tajura lies about 20 km from the metropolitan center eastward along the coast. Janzur lies at the same distance westward, also close to the Mediterranean Sea. Both Bin Ghashir and al-Suwani are more in the interior part of the country, Bin Ghashir lying 25 km south of the center and al-Suwani 25 km southwest of the city center.[4] Three of these suburbs are the principal urban sectors of their respective municipalities while al-Suwani is only the second most important urban sector in the municipality of al-'Aziziya. The main sector, bearing the name of the municipality al-'Aziziya, is very far to the

south of the other regions. It is the administrative center of the municipality and a small market center completely independent from the city
of Tripoli itself. Finally, al-Qarbulli is the main urban center of the
sixth municipality of Greater Tripoli, lying close to the coastal area,
65 km east of the center of the city of Tripoli. Unlike the other urban
regions in the muhafadha, al-Qarbulli "is both too far to be a suburb
served by Tripoli's facilities, and too close to be a completely independent urban entity. At present it is in many ways a depressed community, lacking adequate service facilities for its population."[5]

DEMOGRAPHIC GROWTH OF GREATER TRIPOLI

Greater Tripoli dominates Libya in the way few metropolises
of the world dominate the countries of which they are part. Demographically, one-third of Libya's total population lives within the
administrative boundaries of the city, whereas London, for instance,
has less than one-fourth of the total population of England and Paris
less than one-fifth of France.[6] The 1973 census figure for the total
population of Greater Tripoli was 707,438, with the highest concentration in the municipality of Tripoli itself. The next largest urban center
in Libya is Benghazi, which had in 1973 a population of only 332,333
or less than one-half that of Tripoli.[7] Table 1.3 shows the distribution
of the population in Greater Tripoli according to municipalities, and
one can clearly see which is the most important region in the muhafadha.
Although in terms of area the municipality of Tripoli is the second
smallest of the six municipalities, it contains 77.7 percent of the
total population of Greater Tripoli.[8] Its density in terms of persons
per square kilometer is ten times higher than the next most densely
populated region in the muhafadha and almost one thousand times
higher than the least densely populated municipality of Greater
Tripoli.[9]

The rate of growth for the whole country in general has been
very high both in terms of natural increase and in terms of migration.
The statistics for Tripoli are an interesting example of this growth.
The crude birthrate between 1966 and 1972 shows an expected steady
increase from 31.7 per thousand in 1966 to 53.5 in 1972.[10] The year
1973, however, shows a sharp and inexplicable drop in the birthrate
from 53.5 to 46.5. The same sharp drop in the crude birthrate in
1973 was recorded for Sabha (an almost 9.0 drop), al-Zawiya (an 8.2
drop), Masrata (a 4.6 drop), Benghazi (a 5.3 drop), and Darna (a
5.0 drop). Jabal al-Akhdar, al-Khalij, al-Khums, and Gharyan were
the only muhafadhat that showed a slight increase in crude birthrate.[11]
This sharp drop in 1973 would only be significant if the birthrate continued to decline, or at least stopped rising for the period between
1973 and the present, all over the country.

TABLE 1.3

Population of Greater Tripoli
(by municipality)

Municipality	Population	Area in km^2	Density in Persons per km^2
Al-Qarbulli	15,247	560	27.2
Tajura	34,833	565	61.6
Tripoli	567,836	250	2,271.3
Janzur	31,788	140	227.1
Bin Ghashir	45,511	1,378	33.0
Al-'Aziziya	35,517	789	45.0
Total	730,732	3,682	198.5

Source: Based on Italconsult for the Government of the Libyan Arab Republic, Ministry of Planning and Scientific Research, Settlement Pattern Study, Appendix (Rome, 1976), p. 11.

The crude deathrates for Tripoli during the same period 1966-73 are also rather puzzling and one may wonder at their accuracy. Given the undeniable facts that health care has greatly improved in Libya and has been free for all since 1969, and that education of the younger generation and the adult population has made impressive steps forward, it becomes rather difficult to understand why the crude deathrate should rise over the years rather than decline. Between 1966 and 1970 the difference is a small although significant rise from 3.8 to 5.1 deaths per thousand population. In 1971 the crude deathrate rises to 6.7, jumps to 11.3 in 1972, and falls to 8.4 in 1973.[12] It is interesting to note here that 1972 has both the highest crude birthrate of 53.5 per thousand and the highest crude deathrate of 11.3 per thousand for all that period. The figures appear to be inflated both ways for that year.

When comparing Tripoli's crude birthrates and deathrates for the period 1966-73 with those of the national average a predictable picture emerges. In general, Tripoli's crude birthrate has been roughly the same as that of most other areas in Libya. In 1966, 1967, 1970, and 1971, it was a little below the national average by 2.5 births per thousand, while in 1968, 1969, 1972, and 1973 it was above the national average by roughly 2.9 births per thousand.[13] The crude deathrates in Tripoli during that same period, on the other hand, are consistently lower than the national average (except for the unusual figures of 1972). This is not surprising in view of the fact that health care and health facilities in Libya are much more concentrated in urban areas than in other areas of the country and that Tripoli has the largest share of those facilities.[14] The crude deathrate for that whole period was about 1.6 deaths per thousand lower than the national average.[15]

Migration is another source of increase of the population of Greater Tripoli. It is a major problem of urban growth and warrants extensive research. However, in this chapter we shall only be concerned with the purely statistical aspect of this problem. We shall deal with three facets of the issue: emigration, immigration, and migration or mobility within the muhafadha.

Emigration is a social phenomenon that is almost never discussed where Tripoli is concerned for the simple reason that immigration to, rather than emigration from, Tripoli is the cause of much concern to the administrative authorities of the muhafadha. However, emigration from Tripoli has occurred to some degree, interestingly enough at the same time as extensive immigration to Tripoli began, that is within the last decades. This can be seen in Table 1.4, which shows that the largest age-group born in Tripoli but residing in another muhafadha is the 5 to 9 age-group. In other words, those children and their parents moved within five to nine years before the census of 1973 was taken to another region and out of Tripoli.

Table 1.4 is based on the published and adjusted census results that appeared in 1977-78 concerning the census taking of 1973. It shows a total of more than 8,285 Tripoli migrants (as al-Zawiya results were not published yet when this table was prepared) residing in other muhafadhat. For the period 1954-64 the figure was lower— 5,633.[16] Although the proportion to the total population of Tripoli is not very significant in either case, what is significant is the proportion of the number of migrants from Tripoli to the number of migrants emigrating from other areas. For instance, there were more migrants emigrating from Tripoli, up to 1973, to the muhafadha of Gharyan, than from any other muhafadha in Libya,[17] the reason probably being a geographical one of proximity. However, the migration from Greater Tripoli to the Khalij region is one of the lowest in Libya.[18] On the whole the absolute number of migrants from Tripoli to other regions is an average number when compared to the absolute number of migrants emigrating from other muhafadhat to the various regions of the country, except to Tripoli.

Immigration to Tripoli is a very important problem that faces the muhafadha in its urban growth and development. More than half the Libyans who migrated from one region to another in their lifetime came to Tripoli. Out of 278,460 Libyans who were born in another

TABLE 1.4

Emigration from Tripoli

Muhafadha	Number of Persons Born in Tripoli	Predominant Age-Group
Al-Khalij	284[1]	no predominant age-group
Sabha	606[2]	5-9
Darna	684[3]	5-9
Masrata	652[4]	1-4, 5-9, 10-14
Al-Jabal al-Akhdar	749[5]	5-9
Benghazi	3,442[6]	all age-groups up to 45-49
Gharyan	949[7]	1-4, 5-9
Al-Khums	919[8]	1-4, 5-9, 10-14
Total	8,285	

Note: Only one muhafadha is missing, al-'Aziziya, for which we found no figures.

Sources:

[1]SPLAJ, Secretariat of Planning, Census and Statistics Department, Nata'ij al-Ta'dad al-'Am lil-Sukan, Al Khalij (Tripoli, 1977), Table 69, pp. 123-24.

[2]SPLAJ, Secretariat of Planning, Census and Statistics Department, Nata'ij al-Ta'dad al-'Am lil-Sukan, Sabha (Tripoli, 1977), Table 69, pp. 130-31.

[3]SPLAJ, Secretariat of Planning, Census and Statistics Department, Nata'ij al-Ta'dad al-'Am lil-Sukan, Darna (Tripoli, 1977), Table 69, pp. 122-23.

[4]SPLAJ, Secretariat of Planning, Census and Statistics Department, Nata'ij al-Ta'dad al-'Am lil-Sukan, Masrata (Tripoli, 1977), Table 69, pp. 120-21.

[5]SPLAJ, Secretariat of Planning, Census and Statistics Department, Nata'ij al-Ta'dad al-'Am lil-Sukan, Al-Jabal al-Akhdar (Tripoli, 1977), Table 69, pp. 125-26.

[6]SPLAJ, Secretariat of Planning, Census and Statistics Department, Nata'ij al-Ta'dad al-'Am lil-Sukan, Benghazi (Tripoli, 1977), Table 69, pp. 122-23.

[7]SPLAJ, Secretariat of Planning, Census and Statistics Department, Nata'ij al-Ta'dad al-'Am lil-Sukan, Gharyan (Tripoli, 1977), Table 69, pp. 142-43.

[8]SPLAJ, Secretariat of Planning, Census and Statistics Department, Nata'ij al-Ta'dad al-'Am lil-Sukan, Al-Khums (Tripoli, 1977), Table 69, pp. 120-21.

muhafadha from that of enumeration at the time the census was taken in 1973, 141,386 came to Tripoli. And out of 68,433 Libyans who were born outside Libya (some of whom may originally have been of other Arab nationalities and become Libyan at a later period), 38,700 or more than 56 percent, were residing in Tripoli at the time of the census taking. [19] Migration of non-Libyans to Tripoli was just as striking: out of 196,865 non-Libyans in Libya in 1973, Tripoli alone had 77,760 persons, or 40 percent of their total number. [20] Over and above this figure, there is a large number of illegal migrants, mainly from Tunisia and Egypt, who cross the borders, seeking work in Libya, but are not officially registered with the authorities and probably not reported to the census researchers either. Some estimate the illegal migration to be as high as 10 percent of the total migrant population in Libya, with the proportion being even higher for urban centers where migrants find more work opportunities and a greater degree of anonymity. The largest proportion of non-Libyan legal migrants, roughly 89 percent, is from other Arab countries, while the remaining 11 percent is made up of Europeans, Americans, and a small community of Indians and Pakistanis consisting of 2,695 persons. [21] Both the Arabs and non-Arabs are temporary migrants, usually residing in Tripoli for periods averaging one to five years. [22]

Internal mobility, or migration from one region to another within Greater Tripoli, is a final aspect of the entire issue of migration. Italconsult, an Italian consulting firm that did a survey of Libya, gives some figures for the period 1954-64 based on the Population Census of 1964. The figure for that decade was 33,845 individuals who had moved within the muhafadha, while the net migration in the same period into Greater Tripoli was 26,462. And when one looks at the most recent figures concerning the number of people within Tripoli who moved in their lifetime from one region to another in the same muhafadha, the number rises to 172,100, as compared to 277,468 who were found to be in the same region of their birth. [23] In other words, more than 59 percent of Tripoli's population moved at least once in their lifetime from one region to another within the same administrative unit. As one can note from these figures, Tripoli has a highly mobile population. Migration is the highest in the country, and internal mobility is occurring at a very high rate, too. The implications for urban growth and development of this mobility are far-reaching and shall be dealt with later.

POPULATION CHARACTERISTICS OF GREATER TRIPOLI

The population of Greater Tripoli is representative of the total Libyan population in terms of sex, with a larger proportion of males than females. The census figures show that in 1973 there were 328,364 females to 379,074 males in Tripoli,[24] with figures slightly different from those of the total Libyan population. Whereas there are 8.8 women for every 10 men in Libya, there are 8.6 women for every 10 men in Tripoli, according to the census.[25] The difference here may be due primarily to migration, with a larger proportion of Libyan men migrating to urban centers than women (76,256 males to 65,130 females)[26] in search of work. Migration of non-Libyan men to Tripoli is even higher in comparison to migration of non-Libyan women (51,507 men to 26,253 women), or almost double that of women.[27]

In terms of age-groups, the Libyan population is, as in most developing nations, a very young population. The census has very interesting figures for Greater Tripoli, showing that the two largest age-groups in the population in 1973 were the 5 to 9 age-group with 112,789 individuals and the 10 to 14 age-group with 82,840 persons.[28] When those figures were compared, for instance, with those of the two age-groups between 25 and 29, and between 30 and 34, where the total numbers were 36,750 and 31,380 respectively, the difference is striking.[29] In other words, there were almost three individuals, in 1973, in the age bracket of 5 to 14 for every one individual in the age bracket between 25 to 34. The reasons for this difference are not hard to find: with an increase in the wealth of the Libyans after the discovery of oil, and the tremendous advances made in health care, education, nutrition, and so forth since 1969, infant mortality has decreased sharply, and a much larger number of children are surviving to become adults. As there is no family-planning program as such on the national level, and on the contrary the emphasis is on large families in order to increase the country's small population, there are no social, economic, political, or cultural forces to counterbalance this trend of large families, most of the children of which are surviving under the improved environmental conditions.

The preface to the published census results of 1973 defines urban areas in Libya as "all areas lying within the boundaries of the capital of the municipalities and their sub-sectors or fir ' baladiyas, irrespective of the size of the population living within those areas or the nature of their activities."[30] On the basis of this definition, the portion of the population that is urban in Greater Tripoli is 95.7 percent.[31]

If one were to use one of the most often applied definitions of an urban area to describe the population of the muhafadha of Tripoli the picture might be a little different. In 1956 International Urban Research, an American research team, standardized the definition of an urban area for all countries of the world in order to facilitate comparison. Their definition of an urban area was "an urban unit containing a population of at least 100,000 people, being an area embracing a central city or cities, plus adjacent areas with an economic relationship with that city and with 65 per cent or more of their economically active populations engaged in non-agricultural activities."[32] Under this definition Greater Tripoli is without doubt an urban area with its population of over 700,000 predominantly involved in nonagricultural activities, and having a major city center surrounded by other urban centers related economically and otherwise to the city.

When broken down into its separate municipalities, Greater Tripoli shows a great divergence between one area and another in terms of population density (see Table 1.3) and the nature of the activities of the work force (see Table 1.5). No other region except the municipality of Tripoli has had a population of more than 50,000; and Tripoli and Janzur are the only two municipalities that have 65 percent or more of their work force involved in nonagricultural activities, Tajura being a borderline case. Bin Ghashir, al-Qarbulli, and al- Aziziya have roughly half their work force involved in agricultural activities. If then we were to consider those areas within Greater Tripoli urban, 65 percent of the work force of which would be involved in nonagricultural activities, Tripoli and Janzur would be the only two real urban municipalities in Greater Tripoli. Although, according to the figures, Tajura has only 61 percent of its work force involved in nonagricultural activities, it could be considered urban on the basis that probably the majority of the 4 percent who are categorized in Table 1.5 as unspecified or seeking work for the first time are probably living in urban centers, unemployed, and/or seeking occupations of a nonagricultural nature. Consequently, the total urban population of Greater Tripoli would comprise the sum total of the populations of Tripoli, Janzur, and Tajura, in other words, 633,457 persons or 86.6 percent of the total population of the muhafadha of Tripoli (see Table 1.3). This is a more realistic figure than the census figure of 95.7 percent, and gives a more accurate picture of the proportion of rural-urban population in Greater Tripoli. Those figures (86.6 percent urban, 13.4 percent rural) tally quite nicely with the estimates made by Italconsult concerning the proportion of the total work force of Greater Tripoli that is involved in rural activities, i.e., 13 percent.[33]

Under the definition of urban and rural areas mentioned above, the census includes nomads and seminomads under the category of "rural" population, as their areas of residence fall outside the capitals of the municipalities and their subsectors. They form roughly 0.54 percent of the total population of Greater Tripoli. The census gives the following definitions for these groups:

TABLE 1.5

Activities of the Work Force of Greater Tripoli
(for each municipality)

Municipality	Percentage of Work Force in Agricultural Activities	Percentage of Work Force in Nonagricultural Activities	Percentage of Work Force Unspecified/Seeking Work for the First Time	Total Work Force
Al-Qarbulli	48%	48%	4%	100%
Tajura	35	61	4	100
Tripoli	5	90	5	100
Janzur	28	69	3	100
Bin Ghashir	53	42	5	100
Al-'Aziziya	50	48	2	100

Source: Calculations based on Italconsult for the Libyan Arab Republic, Ministry of Planning and Scientific Research, Settlement Pattern Study, Appendix (Rome, 1976), p. 21, which used unpublished data from the Population Census of 1973, Table F3-02.3.3.

Semi-nomads: are household members who mainly live in tents and lead a bedouin life, always moving within their administrative boundaries from one place to another throughout winter and spring in quest of water and pasturage for their animals. They are tied, at the same time, to certain areas of rain-fed farming which rather restrict their movements. They often do not go beyond their administrative boundaries except in drought years when they are forced to migrate in quest of pasturage for their animals, but often return to their normal place of residence after a short period of time. In summer they live and take lodging in stockades near waterwells to ensure adequate water supply for themselves and their animals. During this period they settle down, and some of them migrate to coastal areas or oases for the palm date harvest.[34]

Nomads: are those who entirely lead a bedouin life; their sole occupation is animal husbandry; they have no farming to restrict their movements. Therefore, they keep wandering in limited groups in remote areas with adequate rainfall and abundant pasturage, even if such areas fall outside the borders of what they deem as their own property. They might stay in such areas for long periods of time which may extend to years without going back to their primary area of residence.[35]

As is apparent by the definition of a nomad, it may be almost impossible to have accurate figures as to their number. First, because of their high mobility, which takes them to regions often inaccessible to a census researcher. Second, as they move in small groups it becomes difficult to keep track of all the small groups spread out over very large areas. Third, the difficulty lies in ascertaining to which area they belong as they move from region to region, not taking into account administrative boundaries and having their own set of territorial boundaries.

Consequently, one could question the census figures given for the nomadic and seminomadic population of 117 male nomads and 99 female nomads, and 1,458 male seminomads and 1,004 female seminomads[36] for the muhafadha of Tripoli. The figures given in terms of households in Table 12 of the Population Census Summary seem to be a more accurate estimate, as information concerning families and households is easier to obtain than information concerning individuals, especially women. The precise number of households may not be accurate (560 for the seminomadic households of Greater

Tripoli and 43 for the nomads),[37] but the percentage this group makes up of the total population of greater Tripoli, 0.54 percent, is probably a close estimate. One reason for this small number, as Italconsult noted, is the very high rate of sedentarization, half the number of nomads having settled over the last ten years in Libya as they have sought and found more remunerative occupations near or in the cities.[38]

IMPLICATIONS OF THIS STUDY FOR TRIPOLI

The extensive concentration of population in one urban center can create major problems for the city and for the country as a whole. Social services, for instance, which are provided by the government, such as health facilities, standard dwelling units, school transportation, and so forth, have had to be very rapidly developed to enable the city to cope with the increase in its population. This in turn has had two net outcomes: first, it has resulted in the concentration of social facilities in Tripoli, to the detriment of other regions in Libya that still suffer from severe shortages in such services; second, it has created a "vicious circle" situation, whereby immigration into the city has accelerated because the social services are better and more available than in other regions of Libya.

The drain in human and material resources has also been a major problem resulting from this lopsided demographic growth in Libya. Whereas, for instance, Tripoli suffers from unemployment at the level of the unskilled worker, most rural areas are suffering from underemployment, and precious arable land is not being cultivated because of a shortage of manpower in the rural hinterland. Furthermore, in order to make use of the existing unemployed manpower, light, medium, and heavy industrial projects have been planned and some have already been set up in Tripoli. This, in turn, has encouraged more rural migrants to come to the city in search of better and more lucrative job opportunities.

Other basic problems that are a result of this rapid demographic growth in Tripoli[39] are: congested traffic in the capital, leading to the need for the development of an improved road system; overcrowded housing conditions in the old section of the city of Tripoli reaching very serious proportion, where families live in homes with no sanitary facilities and in dilapidated condition; overcrowding of schools, especially boys' schools, where building new schools cannot keep up with the increase of the population; extensive use of the water reserves of the city, whereby the natural subterranean water reservoirs are being drained at a faster rate than they can be replenished; increasing security problems as crimes are more easily perpetrated in a crowded city because of its cover of anonymity, necessitating increases in security forces in order to cope with the rising crime rate; and public transportation is insufficient to meet the needs of urban dwellers, and becoming a major problem for those who cannot afford private transport. Thus in Libya, like in most developing countries, the rapid demographic growth of one or two major urban centers polarizes development and is, in the long run, detrimental to the overall economic and social growth of the country.

The population characteristics of the city also have very important developmental implications for Tripoli. With almost half the population under 14 years of age, the problem of education and the development of educational facilities in the city has become one of the major problems of the administration. It appears that at the primary level, at least, school facilities have been constructed not only in Tripoli, but in most parts of Libya as well. However, at the intermediate (or preparatory) and secondary levels much still has to be done in order to meet the educational needs of the youngsters in the city. The problem of teachers is also a very major one as there are not enough suitably trained Libyans to teach this very large and very young population. But we shall deal with these problems later.

Other factors are related to the age of the population of Tripoli. Recreational facilities, for instance, for the young are almost nonexistent and must be made part of the overall planning of the city. Restless, aimless teenagers can become a serious social problem in a fast-growing urban center like Tripoli. Housing units being built in Tripoli are of the modern apartment-type units found in most cities of the world. However, the Libyan family is also one of the largest in the world, and overcrowding of housing units is a problem in Tripoli. The traditional one-family house (which included some members of the extended family) was much more suitable to large families because of the space it provided for growing children. With the overcrowding of the city, such houses have become uneconomical to build. In terms of women's emancipation, a large, young family is a drawback. Whereas in the rural areas children eventually assist their parents in activities, in urban centers children will tend to keep women home and prevent them from becoming more active in the work force.

Finally, as Tripoli is developing at a very rapid pace toward a "modern" type of urban, semiindustrialized center, its nomadic and seminomadic population is becoming "progressively emarginated from an economic and social point of view"[40] from the rest of the society. This in turn is leading to the sedentarization of some of the bedouins, and unfortunately to the gradual loss of much of the cultural traditions of the Libyan society.

These are only some of the problems the Libyan government has to tackle when dealing with the rapid urbanization of Tripoli, and to some extent Benghazi. It will probably have to focus its development strategy on more decentralization, where more emphasis is placed on new agricultural and industrial projects in rural areas and community services are provided in all key towns in the less-developed regions of the country in order to reduce the flow of migration to urban centers.

NOTES

1. For a complete description of the administrative divisions of Greater Tripoli and their boundaries, see the Libyan Arab Republic (LAR), Ministry of Planning, Census and Statistics Department, Al-Dalil al-Jughrafi, Muhafadhat Tarablus (Tripoli: Al-Matba'a al-Libiya, 1973).

2. See the section on tribes and mahallas in Al-Dalil al-Jughrafi.

3. Discussion with Yassin al-Kabir of al-Fateh University, January 1978.

4. Italconsult for the Libyan Arab Republic, Ministry of Planning and Scientific Research, Settlement Pattern Study, Tripoli Region (Rome, 1976), p. 64.

5. Ibid., p. 73.

6. Peter Hall, The World Cities (New York: McGraw-Hill, 1971), p. 23.

7. Socialist People's Libyan Arab Jamahiriya (SPLAJ), Secretariat of Planning, Census and Statistics Department, Population Census Summary Data 1393 AH, 1973 AD (Tripoli, n.d.), Table 2, p. 2.

8. Ibid. See Table 3, p. 7.

9. There is a discrepancy between the census figure for the total population of Greater Tripoli and that of Italconsult. The latter's figure seems to be a somewhat higher estimate or may refer to a later period, although this is not mentioned.

10. LAR, Ministry of Planning and Scientific Research, Department of Census and Statistics, Al-Majmu'a al-Ihsa'iya 1393 AH, 1973 AD (Tripoli: Government Press, 1975), Table 6, p. 45.

11. Ibid., Table 5, p. 44.

12. Ibid.

13. Our calculations are based on Al-Majmu'a al-Ihsa'iya.

14. Ibid., Table 7, p. 59, on the Distribution of General Government and Private Hospitals.

15. Our own calculations.

16. Italconsult for the Libyan Arab Republic, Ministry of Plan-

ning and Scientific Research, Settlement Pattern Study, Appendix (Rome, 1976), Table 18, p. 20.

17. SPLAJ, Secretariat of Planning, Census and Statistics Department, Nata'ij al-Ta'dad al-'Am lil-Sukkan, 1393 AH, 1973 AD, Gharyan (Tripoli: Government Press, 1977), Table 69, p. 143.

18. SPLAJ, Secretariat of Planning, Census and Statistics Department, Nata'ij al-Ta'dad al-'Am lil Sukkan, 1393 AH, 1973 AD, Al-Khalij (Tripoli: Government Press, 1977), Table 69, p. 124.

19. Population Census Summary Data, Table 25, p. 25.

20. Ibid., Table 29, p. 29.

21. Ibid.

22. Ibid., Table 32, p. 32.

23. Ibid., Table 25, p. 25.

24. Ibid., Table 2, p. 2.

25. Calculations are based on Population Census Summary Data. These are the uncorrected figures, before applying the International Labor Office (ILO) formula to adjust the sex ratio.

26. Ibid., Table 25, p. 25.

27. Ibid., Table 16, p. 16.

28. Ibid., Table 16, p. 16.

29. Ibid.

30. SPLAJ, Secretariat of Planning, Census and Statistics Department, Nata'ij al-Ta'dad al-'Am lil-Sukkan, 1393 AH, 1973 AD, Benghazi (Tripoli: Government Press, 1977), p. 3.

31. Population Census Summary Data, Table 3, p. 3.

32. Quoted in Peter Hall, The World Cities, p. 19.

33. Italconsult, Settlement Pattern Study, Appendix, p. viii.

34. English Preface of the Population Census Summary Data, p. 2.

35. Ibid.

36. Ibid., Table 14, p. 14.

37. Ibid., Table 12, p. 12.

38. Italconsult for the Libyan Arab Republic, Ministry of Planning and Scientific Research, Settlement Pattern Study, Gharian Region (Rome, 1976), p. vii.

39. Other problems related to the assimilation of rural migrants in Tripoli have been dealt with in an excellent study by Yassin Ali al-Kabir, "Assimilation of Rural Migrants in Tripoli" (Ph.D. diss., Department of Sociology, Case Western University, Cleveland, January 1972).

40. Italconsult for the Libyan Arab Republic, Ministry of Planning and Scientific Research, Settlement Pattern Study, Summary (Rome, 1976), p. v.

Chapter 2

EDUCATIONAL DEVELOPMENT IN LIBYA
FROM EARLY OTTOMAN TIMES
TO THE PRESENT

INTRODUCTION

This chapter analyzes the development of education in Libya from early Ottoman times to the present, describing the structure of the educational systems in each period and pointing out some of the problems inherent in these systems.

HISTORICAL DEVELOPMENT

Education in the early period of Ottoman rule in Libya (1551–1711) was predominantly religious. There were small Koranic schools attached to major mosques set up by the indigenous population and funded by it where children were sent to learn to read and write and where they were taught to memorize verses from the Qur'an.[1]

There were also religious institutes of higher learning, mainly in Tripoli—such as the Institute of Murad Pasha, attached to the mosque of the same name in Tajura, and the Institute of Darghut Pasha, attached to the Mosque of Darghut Pasha in Tripoli—where the Qur'an and the fiqh (Islamic jurisprudence) were taught.[2] The teachers, men of learning and religion, graduated from those institutes.

The mosques had a third type of educational institution attached to them, the zawiya, an offshoot of the famous North African Marabout religious-military brotherhood of the twelfth and thirteenth centuries. The movement began as a kind of monastic order but soon became wealthy due to the awqaf land and property, given by Libyan and Turkish notables. Although different in many aspects from the

18

original Marabout, the zawiya during that period of Ottoman rule was an even more important institution than the latter two. Not only did it provide teaching, prayer, and hand copying of the Qur'an and other religious manuscripts, but also the teaching of the sciences of astronomy, geography, history, and medicine. [3] Tripoli had three major zawiyas: zawiyat al-Shaykh Abu Rawi and zawiyat al-Na'as in Tajura and zawiyat al-Qa'id 'Amura in Janzur. [4]

Under the Qaramanlis (1711-1835) Libya as a whole, and Tripoli in particular, witnessed a new development in the educational system. Due to the commercial growth and prosperity of that part of the North African continent in the eighteenth and early nineteenth centuries, a large number of Europeans began coming to Libya, in particular French and Italian Jews who set up the first non-Islamic school for their children in 1804 in Tripoli. The languages that were taught were French and Hebrew, and the Bible and the Talmud were the main subjects of education. In 1810, the Franciscans set up the first Christian schools in Tripoli and included mathematics as part of the curriculum. [5] The Qarmanlis set up a new religious institute of higher learning in Tripoli, the famous Ahmad Pasha Institute, active to this day, in which religion was taught as well as history, geography, and some of the sciences. [6]

In the period of the second Ottoman occupation (1835-1911) changes began to take place at a faster pace. First, the zawiya began to acquire greater importance in Libya when Muhammad 'Ali ibn Sanusi, the founder of the famous Sanusi movement, decided to set up the first Sanusi zawiya at Barqa in 1843. Begun as a religious and educational movement, it soon became social and political. [7] On the educational level it had a hierarchical structure comprised of the scholars who lectured at the various schools and institutes of the Sanusi zawiyas and who formed a kind of council called Majlis al-Ikhwan. Next were the elders of the zawiyas, some of whom were part of the council, or majlis. Last was a group made up of the young graduates of the Sanusi institutes whose main functions were social and economic, namely, to get the support and commitment of the tribes around them and to involve themselves in commerce and trade with zawiya members in various regions. [8] Each zawiya in turn was headed by a shaykh, his assistant, and a council that included the tribal notables as well as the religious figures of the tribes. The zawiyas spread during that period from being originally limited to the mosque and its immediate neighborhood at the early stages to large geographic areas with regional boundaries. Their number increased tremendously, reaching 95 by the end of the nineteenth century. [9] The instructional program during that era included (apart from the traditional religious teachings) a new element—applied

military sciences. It is clear that the goals of the Sanusi movement
were not only educational but primarily religious and political.

In the latter part of the nineteenth century, Tripoli was again
the center of a new development in the educational system of the
country. Under the enlightened rule of Muhammad Hafiz Pasha, the
Ottoman Wali governor of Tripoli, modern education in Libya may
be said to have begun. Two primary schools for boys were opened
and one for girls. A training school for teachers was set up and,
most important, vocational schools for the manufacturing of shoes,
silk, and for carpentry and printing were opened in Tripoli. A school
for young boys and girls was also opened in which they were taught
to weave carpets. [10]

Education in Tripoli came through yet another channel: the
military. In 1888, the Ottomans created a military school in Tripoli
under the supervision of the Ministry of Defence in Istanbul. It included a five-year internship in Libya and six more years of study
in Istanbul, after which the graduates became officers in the Ottoman
army. [11] The program, taught in Turkish, included the sciences related to artillery, military engineering, mathematics, and the natural
sciences as well as some history and geography. [12] All these were
"modern" sciences and should be viewed as such in terms of their
developmental impact on the educational system in Libya.

Finally, there was another type of educational institution that
began to grow primarily in Tripoli but also in other regions of Libya
as well. This was the foreign school, generally either Jewish or
Catholic. The process had already started under the Qaramanlis,
but became more prominent after the second half of the nineteenth
century. For instance, Le Bon Pasteur school in 1846 opened a girls'
school for Christian, Muslim, and Jewish girls (who numbered 60)
where Italian was the language of instruction and music part of the
curriculum. In 1876 an Italian primary school was opened mainly for
young Italian boys while another school set up by Franciscan friars
in 1881 co-opted many of the sons of Turkish officers and taught them
both Italian and French. However, by 1888 the Italian government
became involved in the spread of education in Libya and opened several schools for boys and girls with programs in Italian used in the
schools in Italy. [13] In 1901, the Jewish community opened yet another
school, the Alliance Israelite Universelle, made up of two sections:
one for boys and one for girls. Several languages were taught there
as well as geography, arithmetic, accounting, and some manual vocational training. By 1902 they already had 65 students. [14] Table 2.1
shows the schools in Tripoli in 1902.

The Italian colonial period saw a new era in the development of
education in Libya. Although at first sight it may appear to have
greatly improved the situation, the reality behind the figures is very

TABLE 2.1

Schools in Tripoli in 1902

Type of School	Number of Teachers	Number of Students
Primary school for boys	3	132
Primary school for girls	3	160
Intermediary school for boys	6	70
Teachers' training institute	2	20
Military school	10	150
Arts and crafts school	4	65
Charity institution	7	100
French school	—*	150
Jewish school	—	125
Italian school	—	46

*Data not available.

Note: These figures do not include the Koranic schools, the zawiyas, or other Islamic institutions of learning.

Source: Based on the figures in Rif'at Ghanami Al-Shaykh, Tatawwur al-Ta'lim fi Libya fi al-'Usur al-Haditha (Benghazi: Dar al-Tanmiya lil-Nashr wal-Tawzi', 1972), pp. 85-86.

different. A. J. Steele-Greig, the chief education officer in the British Military Administration in the 1940s, wrote two reports on the development of education under the Italian and the British administrations in Libya that provide some insights as well as statistics on the educational system in Libya in the first half of the twentieth century. Table 2.2 shows some of the trends during the Italian colonial period. One can note, first, that the total number of schools increased tremendously between 1921 and 1939; second, the total number of students increased almost tenfold during that period; third, Italian and Jewish schools became very significant both in number and importance; and finally, the Libyan schools and student body increased very rapidly as well.

However, in another section of that same appendix to Steele-Greig's work some important qualifications to the four points mentioned above emerge: first, there were no secondary schools for Libyans, although Italians had up to eight secondary schools in 1934-35; second, out of a total of 16,246 Arab students during the

TABLE 2.2

Number of Schools, Pupils, and Teachers in Libya
for Selected Years from 1921 to 1939

Type of School	Number of Schools				
	1921-22	1925-26	1930-31	1934-35	1938-39
Italian	10	20	38	65	93
Arab	56	89	303	560	418
Jewish	3	7	6	18	16
Greek		1	1	1	1
Total	69	117	348	644	528
	Number of Pupils				
Italian	2,173	2,724	3,306	7,715	7,344
Arab	2,559	7,396	9,942	16,246	15,497
Jewish	1,076	2,952	2,572	4,744	5,451
Greek		56	58	39	16
Total	5,808	13,128	15,878	24,744	28,308
	Number of Teachers				
Italian	322	333	227	370	612
Arab	36	70	69	90	125
Jewish	—	—	—	—	—
Greek	1	2	2	2	2
Total	359	405	298	462	797

Note: Dash indicates information not available.
Source: A. J. Steele-Greig, A Short History of Education in
Tripolitania (Tripolitania: Department of Education, 1947), Appendix
6, p. 35.

academic year 1934-35, 9,864 or over 60 percent were in private
Koranic schools; and third, out of the 560 Libyan schools in that same
year of 1934-35, 503 schools or 89.8 percent of the total were Koranic
schools.[15] (See Table 2.3.)

In other words, what at first sight appeared to have been an
achievement of the Italian rule gives a completely different picture
when broken down to its various parts. It is our belief that the local
population in Libya reacted to the forced "Italianization" of the

TABLE 2.3

Type and Number of Schools, Number of Pupils, and Number
of Teachers in Libya for Selected Years from 1921 to 1939

Type of School	Number of Schools				
	1921-22	1925-26	1930-31	1934-35	1938-39
Secondary					
Italian	1	3	5	8	5
Arab	—	—	—	—	1[a]
Jewish	—	—	—	—	—
Total	1	3	5	8	6
Trade and Technical					
Italian	1	1	2	3	3
Arab	—	—	1	5[b]	5
Jewish	—	—	—	—	—
Total	1	1	3	8	8
Statal					
Italian	4	10	24	42	72
Arab	4	18	34	52	64
Jewish	2	5	5	2	2
Primary Parastatal					
Italian	4	6	7	5	7
Arab	—	—	—	—	—
Jewish	—	—	—	—	—
Primary Private[c]					
Italian	—	—	—	7	6
Arab	52[d]	69[d]	260[d]	503[d]	348[d]
Jewish	1	2	1	16[e]	14[e]
Total	67	111	332	628	514
	Number of Pupils				
Secondary					
Italian	270	342	334	1,435	1,417
Arab	6	7	5	20	134
Jewish	66	93	27	64	66
Total	342	442	336	1,519	1,617

(continued)

23

Type of School	1921-22	1925-26	1930-31	1934-35	1938-39
	Number of Pupils (continued)				
Trade and Technical					
Italian	45	45	127	412	382
Arab	150	371	449	522	636
Jewish	48	31	148	32	47
Total	243	447	724	966	1,065
Statal					
Italian	1,621	1,622	2,924	4,665	4,626
Arab	611	142	6,390	5,818	6,736
Jewish	742	1,548	2,136	2,741	3,998
Primary Parastatal					
Italian	237	715	921	740	671
Arab	—	22	33	22	18
Jewish	—	69	75	49	37
Primary Private[c]					
Italian	—	—	—	463	248
Arab	1,792	5,570	5,555	9,864	7,973
Jewish	220	1,211	186	1,858	1,303
Total	5,223	12,239	15,788	26,259	25,626
	Number of Teachers				
Secondary					
Italian	51	47	40	56	54
Arab	—	—	—	—	7
Jewish	—	—	—	—	—
Total	51	47	40	56	61
Trade and Technical					
Italian	23	57	36	40	48
Arab	5	10	10	10	14
Jewish	—	—	—	—	—
Total	28	67	46	50	62
Statal					
Italian	122	202	151	274	487
Arab	31	60	59	80	104
Jewish	—	—	—	—	—

(continued)

TABLE 2.3, continued

Type of School	1921-22	1925-26	1930-31	1934-35	1938-39
Primary Parastatal					
Italian	26	27	—	—	23
Arab	—	—	—	—	—
Jewish	—	—	—	—	—
Primary Private[c]					
Italian	—	—	—	—	—
Arab	—	—	—	—	—
Jewish	—	—	—	—	—
Total	180	291	212	356	674

[a]Superior Islamic school.

[b]These are mostly girls' schools.

[c]Not under control of the Education Department.

[d]Koranic schools.

[e]Rabbinical schools and the Alliance Francaise Jewish schools.

Note: Dash indicates information not available.

Source: A. J. Steele-Greig, A Short History of Education in Tripolitania (Tripolitania: Department of Education, 1947), Appendix 6, p. 35.

colonial educator by opening as many katatib or Koranic schools as possible, funded by its own personal wealth, to educate Libyan children and preserve their religion, language, and cultural heritage through those institutions.

The same can be said of the syllabus taught in the non-Koranic Arab schools in Libya. Although at first sight it appears to be a very modern one including mathematics, history, geography, science, hygiene, and so forth,[16] we find in another report that when the British entered Libya in 1943, "The only book for the use of Arab scholars was a primer for the first class. There were no Arab text-books on arithmetic, history, geography, etc., nor any copies of the Koran. . . ."[17] The latter statement is probably an exaggeration, but the problem is clear: whereas the Italian children received a modern education, Libyan children were either left to follow traditional forms of education or else those few who were incorporated in the "modern" schools were "Italianized" through a program where nothing was taught in Arabic. Steele-Greig, quoting Italian sources, stated, "The Fascist aim was 'to catch them young,' and in instructions issued it was pointed out that it would be difficult to root out old traditions and instil new ones: adults could not be changed; the young could. There-fore 'you must concentrate on the young and emphasis must be given to 'Italianization.' Teach them to break away from native customs, and create in them a knowledge of their new country, its greatness, its glory. Teach them to be proud of being Italians.' So were the teachers instructed."[18] This quotation, from an impartial source, speaks for itself.

By 1940 virtually all the schools had closed down in Libya due to the war and remained so until 1943. Most Italian teachers and many of the pupils had returned to Italy. A number of the Jewish teachers were either put in concentration camps by the Italian govern-ment or else sent to Germany. When the British entered Libya in 1943 while the war was still going on, they were not able to improve the situation substantially, in part "due to the fact that the [British] Ad-ministration is only a temporary body whose terms of reference are 'care and maintenance'"[19] and because the war was still going on.

However, improvements did take place. In 1944 a two-year course for training women as teachers began in Tripoli, with 76 women enrolled in the first year and 77 in the second. [20] Girls' pri-mary schools began to reopen in Tripoli that same year. In 1945 an Arab textbook began to be compiled on the history and geography of Tripolitania. [21] And in 1946 a secondary school for boys opened in Tripoli with 81 boys and an Arab headmaster, 'Abd al-Hakim al-Jamil. A year later the enrollment had jumped to 170 boys. [22] A "Trainee Scheme" was started to prepare young Libyan men to occupy positions in all administrative branches of the government hitherto reserved for Italians, such as the Departments of Agriculture, Customs, Finance, Education, Public Works, and others.

Steele-Greig omits to mention that such changes in the educa-tional system had been demanded by the Libyans themselves in a petition resulting from a demonstration in Tripoli in August 1943 and presented to Brigadier T. R. Blackley, who became chief adminis-trator of Tripolitania during the whole of the British military admin-istration. Majid Khadduri, quoting a British source, stated, "The petition lamented the fact that Tripolitania was still treated as an enemy territory and that high Italian officials were working in depart-ments dealing with native affairs; it asked for the employment of more native officials and equal salaries . . . and the opening of pri-mary schools for Moslems."[23] We thus find the educational system in Tripoli, in particular, as well as in the rest of the country making a new start by the end of World War II and moving slowly but surely in the direction of modernism (see Table 2.4).

By 1951 a UNESCO commission came to Libya to report on the state of education in Libya and then presented its report with some recommendations. R. L. Le Tourneau, one of the members of this

TABLE 2.4

Type and Number of Schools, Number of Pupils,
and Number of Teachers in Tripoli City, 1943–47

Type of School	Number of Schools			
	1943–44	1944–45	1945–46	1946–47
Arab	6	9	11	12
Jewish	—	—	2	2
Italian	8	13	14	16
British	—	—	1	1
Total	14	22	28	32
	Number of Pupils			
Arab	1,543	2,235	2,874	3,308
Jewish	1,146	2,643	3,994	3,945
Italian	2,213	1,920	2,292	3,484
British	—	—	313	276
Total	4,902	6,798	9,473	11,013
	Number of Teachers			
Arab	52	78	83	97
Jewish	—	—	—	—
Italian	115	164	167	167
British	—	—	7	8
Total	167	242	257	272

Note: Dash indicates information not available.
Source: A. J. Steele-Greig, A Short History of Education in
Tripolitania (Tripolitania: Department of Education, 1947), Appendix
7, p. 36.

commission, reported the following concerning the educational situation on the eve of independence. First, primary Libyan schools
were of two kinds: schools with six classes where children could
complete their primary education and schools with up to five classes
only. [24] There were 16 primary schools in the city of Tripoli and 13
in Suq al-Jum'a, then considered outside the boundaries of the city.
There were only two secondary schools in Libya: one in Tripoli and
one in Zawiya. The school in Tripoli had 388 boys and 33 teachers.
There was also a teachers' training center for women in Tripoli

headed by a Palestinian woman that had 89 trainees. It included a two-year program and was "the only educational establishment where really effective school medical service exists."[25] Italian schools were still flourishing and vastly outnumbered the Libyan schools: there were 22 nursery schools, 72 primary schools, and 7 secondary schools in Libya,[26] most of which were in and around Tripoli. Unlike other schools, they followed the official Italian curriculum. There were also five Jewish schools in 1948, three in 1950, and only one by 1951 after the majority of the Jews of Libya emigrated to Israel. The curriculum was based on the Egyptian syllabus in the primary schools of Tripoli and included Koranic and religious studies, Arabic language, music, arithmetic, geometry, history, civics, geography, natural sciences, hygiene, drawing, and so forth.[27] The Tripoli Teachers' Training Center also had a modern syllabus that included religion, Arabic, English, mathematics, physics, chemistry, biology, history, geography, civics, agriculture, physical education, drawing, and educational theory.[28]

Libya's educational system had improved somewhat by the end of the British Military Administration but was still very weak. Ninety percent of the population was illiterate, there were no secondary schools for girls (apart from the teachers' training center), only 14 Libyans had received university degrees, mostly from Egypt, and there remained an urgent need for teachers and for more schools at all levels of education.[29]

When Libya became an independent sovereign monarchical state in 1951, a constitution was prepared with three articles on education that stated:

Article 28: Every Libyan shall have the right to education. The State shall ensure the diffusion of education by means of the establishment of public schools and of private schools which it may permit to be established under its supervision, for Libyans and foreigners.

Article 29: Teaching shall be unrestricted so long as it does not constitute a breach of public order and is not contrary to morality. Public education shall be regulated by law.

Article 30: Elementary education shall be compulsory for Libyan children of both sexes; elementary and primary education in the public schools shall be free.[30]

Those articles can be considered the foundation of the system of modern education in Libya. From that date onward tremendous steps were made to build schools, train teachers, teach children and adults, and so forth.

TABLE 2.5

Education of Women in Libya, 1955–61; number of students

School Year	Primary School	Intermediate School	Secondary School	Teachers' Training Institute	University	Total
1955–56	11,195	25	29	198	—	11,447
1956–57	13,708	78	20	252	—	14,058
1957–58	16,769	127	74	287	1	17,258
1958–59	16,438	182	45	275	6	16,946
1959–60	21,828	305	87	297	13	22,530
1960–61	25,872	472	125	375	18	26,862

Note: Dash indicates zero.
Source: Research Center, University of Benghazi, Lamha 'an al-Wadi' al-Iqtisadi wal-Ijtima'i lil-Mar'a fi al-Jumhuriya al-'Arabiya al-Libiya (Benghazi, 1975), Table 2, p. 20; Table 3, p. 21.

TABLE 2.6

Number of Schools and Students in Libya, 1960-67

Type of School	1960-61 School	1960-61 Pupil	1961-62 School	1961-62 Pupil	1962-63 School	1962-63 Pupil	1963-64 School	1963-64 Pupil	1964-65 School	1964-65 Pupil	1965-66 School	1965-66 Pupil	1966-67 School	1966-67 Pupil
Kindergarten	18	—	17	717	14	1,414	3	640	3	730	3	739	2	510
Primary	558	—	619	131,098	663	144,511	698	153,952	747	170,188	775	189,774	862	215,841
Intermediate	75	—	82	11,189	100	14,691	101	17,548	107	17,711	115	18,720	125	22,038
Secondary	16	—	16	2,283	14	2,708	15	3,092	18	3,760	21	4,326	21	4,808
Technical	11	—	11	1,155	11	1,497	10	1,190	11	1,016	11	933	11	1,064
Teachers' training	11	—	11	2,162	13	2,295	15	2,407	16	2,401	22	3,330	23	4,681
Total	689	—	756	149,604	815	167,116	842	178,829	902	195,806	947	217,822	1,044	248,942

Note: Dash indicates information not available.

Source: Table based on figures in Kingdom of Libya, Ministry of Planning and Development, Census and Statistical Department, Statistical Abstract 1967 (Tripoli, 1968), Table 7, p. 56, and Table 8, p. 57.

The major achievement of the 1950s was the founding of the first Libyan university on December 15, 1955. The first department that was opened was the Arts and Education department in Benghazi.[31] In 1957 the Faculty of Commerce opened and was followed in 1962 by the Law School at the university in Benghazi. In 1966 the College of Agriculture opened in Tripoli, followed in 1967 by the Higher Institute of Arts and the Teachers' Training College, which were incorporated into the university of Tripoli and eventually changed their names to the Colleges of Engineering and Education respectively.[32]

Another major step forward was made during this time in the education of women. As one can note in Table 2.5, the number of women in schools and universities doubled in five years. Even more interesting is the slow but steady increase in female education beyond primary school. For instance, the proportion of women in intermediary classes was almost 19 times higher in 1960-61 than in 1955-56 and 12 times higher in 1959-60 than in the mid-1950s.

Primary and secondary government schools mushroomed all over the country, although in greater numbers in Tripoli and Benghazi. By the late 1950s (1958-59) there were already 14 kindergartens, 473 primary schools, 48 intermediary schools, 13 secondary schools, 11 technical schools, and 8 teachers' training centers in Libya.[33]

The 1960s were a continuation of this trend. However, although education continued to develop at all stages there was a general slowdown, particularly during the academic years between 1961 and 1964 (see Table 2.6).

According to one source, "There was also no great importance attached to vocational and technical education . . . the Libyan University and schools were only meant to prepare a large number of young people for clerical and administrative posts."[34] This is obvious when one looks at the statistics in Table 2.6 and sees that the number of technical schools throughout the period 1960-67 remained the same, and even declined slightly between 1963 and 1964.

Although the number of primary schools increased by 304 schools during that period (1960-67), secondary schools increased only by 5 schools! And between 1962 and 1964 their number went even below the original 16 schools of 1960-61.

Koranic schools and other primary religious schools on the other hand rose in number during the 1960s from 93 in 1965-66 to 125 two years later in 1967-68, with a student body of over 10,000 in 1968-69.[35]

Although teachers' training centers increased during those seven years, the student body only began increasing significantly during the academic year 1965-66. Before that—and although five new training centers had been set up—the number of student trainees remained almost at a standstill (see Table 2.6).

From this brief survey of education under the monarchy, it becomes clear that the foundation for a modern system of education had been laid then and the right of every Libyan to get an education was ensured by the Constitution. Major achievements were made during those 18 years in setting up two universities, encouraging women to get an education, and increasing the number of schools at all levels. However, there still remained very basic problems in the educational system: First, 86.7 percent of the total school population in 1967 was in primary schools; second, technical education had not been encouraged nor were teachers' training centers instructing enough Libyans, with the result that schools were relying more and more heavily on non-Libyan teachers; and finally, small primary Koranic schools with traditional syllabi were attracting an increasing number of students every year.

EDUCATIONAL DEVELOPMENT
SINCE THE REVOLUTION

As a reaction to the above-mentioned problems, the new regime decided to change the educational system to meet Libya's long-term and short-term needs in the most effective way. The government's policies took the following direction:

1. A stress on vocational and technical training to provide the country with the most needed skill in such fields as agriculture, industry, and business;

2. A new trend in higher learning (college and graduate) toward applied sciences with immediate usefulness in the Libyan economy (engineering, petroleum industry, agriculture, medicine, electronics, and others);

3. An increase in the compulsory education period from six to nine years of successful schooling, and changes in the requirements and teaching methods at this level;

4. An expansion of the number and geographical distribution of schools and other educational institutions, in order to bring the rural and Bedouin population in contact with education;

5. A merging between secular and religious education, for example, the amalgamation of the Islamic University with the University of Benghazi;

6. A tremendous increase in adult education under new systems and rules.[36]

With these aims in mind the school system was developed further. In the early 1970s the structure of the system was similar to that in the previous period but important changes had been introduced at all levels. Schools at the primary level were increased in number and became compulsory for all children in Libya. Primary school was composed of six classes, beginning with pupils aged 6 at the first primary and ending with students between ages 12 and 14. At the end of this stage, pupils sat for an exam to obtain their certificate of primary education. The intermediate level of education became compulsory since the revolution for both males and females, and included three years of study only. In order to enter this stage in the educational system a pupil had to be under age 15 and have completed his primary stage of education. Only if there were vacancies by the beginning of the year was a pupil over age 15 accepted in day schools (at the intermediate level). However, older students attending night schools could obtain the same certificate of intermediate education upon passing the required examinations.

The third level of education is secondary education, comprising three years of study, after which students sit for national examinations (i.e., examinations prepared by a committee of teachers at the national level who set the questions for all schools in Libya). Students can then obtain their high school diplomas with which they can enter a university. Education at this level is not compulsory as it is at the other two levels. And although the first year at the secondary level includes a comprehensive program of study, the second and third secondary classes are divided into two sections: the Science section and the Humanities section, with different programs, one section emphasizing sciences and mathematics and the other the humanities and the social sciences (see Table 2.7).

The fourth level of education is the Teachers' Training Program. This system of study is divided into two major categories. The first includes the specialized institutions, which include a four-year program of study after the intermediate stage of schooling where students specialize in certain fields of teaching, such as religion and language, mathematics and sciences, education and music, English literature and language, arts and athletics. The second category of the Teachers' Training Program is available in the schools for general education, which are further subdivided into three categories. First, two-year training schools for teachers include a two-year program after completion of the intermediate school level and students must be at least 15 years old. Second, four-year training schools for teachers include a four-year general program of study. The student must have completed his primary education only before being accepted. (This stage of training, however, was discontinued.) Third, five-year teachers' training programs similar to the previous program require students to have completed their primary education only and be at least 13 years old. As in the other categories, a student does not

TABLE 2.7

Programs Taught at the Secondary Level in All Public Schools
in Libya since the Revolution

First Secondary	Second Secondary	
	Science Section	Humanities Section
Religious Education	Religious Education	Religious Education
Arabic	Arabic	Arabic
English	English	English
French	French	French
Mathematics	Planning for	Planning for
Physics	Development	Development
Chemistry	Mathematics (Algebra,	Geography
Biology	Geometry, Trigo-	History
Geography	nometry)	Philosophy
History	Mechanics	Sociology
Civics	Physics	
Art	Chemistry	
	Biology	

Note: The program of the third secondary includes all the subjects of the second secondary (both sections) except for statistics,
which was added to the Science section.

Source: SPLAJ, Secretariat for Culture and Education, Center
for Educational Research and Documentation, Tashri'at al-Ta'lim
fi al-Jamahiriya al-'Arabiya al-Libiya al-Sha'biya al-Ishtirakiya
1389-1394 AH, 1969-1974 AD (Tripoli, 1977), pp. 433-36.

specialize in any one field but acquires a general education that en-
ables teaching any subject at the primary level. The short-term aim
of those general training schools was to fill in the much-needed
vacancies in all the new schools that were being built and filled with
students. The urgency of this was felt particularly in the peripheral
and rural areas where teachers were much needed.

The fifth level of education is vocational training. This in turn
is divided into two categories. The intermediate stage includes a
four-year program after primary school and comprises courses in
commerce, industry, and agriculture. However, since 1972 new students have not been accepted and the program was eventually discontinued. The other category of training is the secondary stage program,

which requires the student to have obtained his certificate of intermediate education before being accepted. It is a four-year program
and the general courses include commerce, industry, and agriculture
as well as applied engineering. However, during the last three years
of this program a student must decide to become either a mechanic,
blacksmith or welder, auto repairman, electrician, or carpenter.[37]

GROWTH OF THE SCHOOL SYSTEM SINCE 1969

Table 2.8 shows the development and growth of the school system between the academic years 1969-70 and 1975-76. Some very
important facts emerge from this table. First, of the total population
between the ages of 5 and 14 in 1972-73, 71.7 percent attended primary school. A margin of error should be included as most daytime
students enrolled in primary schools are between the ages of 6 and
13; however, there are also students above the age of 15 who attend
primary school at night and are included in the statistics on primary
education. Consequently, in the absence of more accurate figures,
71.7 percent should be taken as an adequate estimate of the number
of children attending primary school as compared to their age-group
in the population.

Second, of the total population between and ages of 15 and 19,
32.2 percent attended intermediate and secondary schools. A margin
of error should also be included here as the majority of students in
intermediate and secondary education fall into the 13-19 age-group.
However, here too there is an unspecified number of older students
attending both night school and day school in order to obtain their
secondary school certificate. The figure 32.2 percent should therefore be taken as an estimate only; the real figure probably is closer
to 36 percent.

Third, a trend that is apparent in those figures is the very
important increase in the number of both intermediate and secondary
schools. At the intermediate stage, for instance, schools increased
by 179.6 percent between 1969-70 and 1975-76, while secondary
schools increased by 133.3 percent during that same period.

Fourth, the number of teachers' training schools, on the other
hand, appears to have remained almost static up to 1972, and then
suddenly jumped in the academic year 1972-73 from 20 schools to 77,
or a 385 percent rise in just one year. The increase in the student
body, however, was less dramatic, rising by only 184 percent.

Finally, although one of the major goals set out by the revolutionary regime was to emphasize vocational training, there seems
to have been little done in this direction. As is apparent from the
figures, there were 12 such vocational schools in the academic year

TABLE 2.8

Number of Schools and Students in Libya, 1969-76

Type of School	1969-70		1970-71		1971-72		1972-73		1973-74		1974-75		1975-76	
	School	Pupil	School	Pupil	School	Pupil	School	Pupil	School	Pupil	School	Pupil	School	Pupil
Primary	1,224	310,846	1,311	348,371	1,397	405,435	1,687	451,928	1,807	484,986	1,906	515,881	1,975	554,015
Intermediate	172	36,316	185	37,047	198	43,346	230	54,744	366	73,928	420	90,463	481	125,432
Secondary	30	8,304	30	8,260	36	9,426	44	10,908	61	13,471	68	14,680	70	18,158
Teachers' training	16	4,725	16	5,377	20	5,984	77	10,990	77	15,606	90	19,546	88	21,377
Technical	12	1,457	14	3,088	15	3,202	14	3,375	12	3,411	13	2,883	12	3,584
Total	1,454	361,648	1,556	402,143	1,666	467,393	2,052	531,945	2,323	591,402	2,497	643,453	2,626	722,566

Source: Libyan Arab Republic, Ministry of Culture and Education, Taqrir 'an Qita' al-Ta'lim wal-Tarbiya min 68/69 ila 1975, pamphlet (n.p., n.d.), tables on pp. 11, 12; see also Ihsa'at al-Ta'lim fi al-Jumhuriya al-'Arabiya al-Libiya 'an al-'Am al-Dirasi 1394-1395 AH, 1974-1975 AD (Tripoli: Government Press, n.d.), pp. 38, 66, 94.

1969-70, and exactly the same number in 1975-76, although the number of students more than doubled during that period. It is not clear why vocational schools that seemed to increase in number until 1971-72 stopped doing so later. Another interesting feature is that the student body actually doubled over one year, i.e., between 1969-70 and 1970-71, at the time when two more schools were added. In other words, there is no consistent pattern either in the rate of increase or decrease of vocational schools, or their student body during that six-year period.

RELIGIOUS EDUCATION

Religous education, the main form of education in the past in Libya, naturally declined in importance with the growth of the modern public schools. However, it is still today a presence to be felt in the education system, and although Koranic schools and Islamic institutes of higher learning have not grown at the same rate as other schools, they still have developed a little since 1968-69.

Between 1968-69 and 1974-75, primary Koranic schools increased from 144 to 181, or by 25.6 percent. The number of students rose from 10,157 to 15,303 during that same period, or an increase of 50.7 percent. The number of teachers, however, increased almost at the same rate as those in public primary schools by almost 108 percent. [38]

At the intermediate level, Islamic institutes grew at a lower rate: there were 8 such schools in 1970-71 and only 12 by 1975. The student body, however, almost doubled from 376 in 1970-71 to 674 in 1975. [39] These institutes were already for older students and are geographically spread all over Libya. They include the institutes of ' Umar ibn al-Khattab in Zawiya, Malik ibn Ans in Tripoli, the Religious Institute of Gharyan, Abi Dhir al-Ghafari in Khums, Al-Asmari al-Dini in Zlaytin, Al-Quwayri al-Dini in Masarata, Zayd bin Thabit and Ibn Ruwaym in the Khalij, Ras ' Ubayda in Benghazi, Malik ibn Ans in al-Gayda, Ma'had Sabha al-Dini in Sabha, and Ma'had Sabha in al-Jaghbub. [40]

What is interesting to note here is that growth has not been equal in all areas or at all stages of religious education. In fact, many institutes actually lost students over the years since the revolution. So although the total number of students has increased, it has done so at different rates in different regions of the country and at different levels of education.

Table 2.9 shows that between 1970 and 1975 religious institutes in Tripoli made substantial gains in the number of students enrolled at the intermediate level—from 155 to 227 in those five years. How-

TABLE 2.9

Number of Students in Intermediate and Secondary Islamic Institutions by Geographical Distribution, 1970-75

Muhafadha	1970-71 Intermediate	Secondary	1971-72 Intermediate	Secondary	1972-73 Intermediate	Secondary	1973-74 Intermediate	Secondary	1974-75 Intermediate	Secondary
Beida	79	98	97	95	84	63	74	23	49	23
Tripoli	155	128	123	126	117	84	219	80	227	76
Zleiten	60	48	77	42	85	34	88	16	92	25
Sabha	20	—	17	—	12	—	11	—	15	—
Gharyan	18	—	27	—	27	—	31	—	38	—
Darna	—	—	—	—	—	—	3	—	—	—
Benghazi	—	—	—	—	—	—	10	—	7	—
Jarbub	—	—	—	—	—	—	—	—	13	—
Zawia	62	—	77	—	74	—	78	—	62	11
Misrata	39	35	52	9	58	5	93	7	82	27
Tarhuna	—	—	—	—	—	—	—	—	—	—
Khums	—	—	23	—	36	—	72	—	69	—
Al-Khalij	—	—	—	—	—	—	10	—	20	—

Note: Dash indicates information not available.

Source: For 1970-71 and 1971-72 figures, Libyan Arab Republic, Al-Majmu'a al-Ihsa'iya 1391 AH, 1971 AD (Tripoli, 1973), p. 95; for 1972-73, Al Majmu'a al-Ihsa'iya 1393 AH, 1973 AD (Tripoli: Government Press, 1975); for 1973-74 and 1974-75, Al-Majmu'a al-Ihsa'iya 1394 AH, 1974 AD (Tripoli, 1976).

ever, at the secondary level they lost almost 40 percent of their student body. In Beida, the trend for both intermediate and secondary schools has been downward, with a net loss at both levels. In Zleiten and Misrata, the trend was similar to that of Tripoli with an increase in students at the intermediate level of religious education and a loss of students at the secondary level. In the regions where there were only intermediate religious schools, the student body doubled, as in Gharyan. But in Zawia although the trend was upward until 1974, it fell back in 1975 to its original level of 1970. Only in Khums has the student body at the intermediate level tripled and yet there are signs that the trend may be going downward in the coming years.[41] Two new institutes were set up in the Khalij regions in 1973-74, the Zayed bin Thabit Institute and the Ibn Ruwaym Institute. However, it is too early as yet to note what the trends will be in that region.

In conclusion, it appears that religious education at the primary level for both girls and boys is growing steadily (though not at a comparable rate to the growth in public schools). The growth at the intermediate level is much slower although the trend is also upward.[42] And finally, at the secondary level there is a marked decline in the student enrollment. (There were only 162 students at the secondary level in religious institutions between 1974-75.) One of the reasons for this may be the greater options for employment in the market and the opportunities for work in the fields of agriculture, industry, medicine, business, engineering, and so forth. Jobs for men of religion are much fewer, as they are now being replaced by the secular school teachers, bureaucrats in the administration, and so forth.

Another reason for these trends may be the merging of religious and secular institutions that enable students to continue their Islamic training while at the same time following a modern system of education. However, the change in compulsory education from merely completing primary school to completing the intermediate levels as well leaves little time for pupils to follow an independent training in religion as well in another institution.

Finally, the changing values of the society have made families at all levels of the social strata desire their children to obtain a modern education in secular schools. Secular education is now not only a means to a higher standard of living (via university training), but also brings with it prestige and social standing.

UNIVERSITY EDUCATION

The universities in Tripoli and Benghazi were founded under the Sanusi monarchy. They continued to expand after the revolution, and in 1970 the Faculty of Medicine was opened in Benghazi and the

Institutes of the Islamic University joined the Libyan University in Beida. The opening of the Faculties of Economics and Commerce as well as those of Science and Petroleum followed in 1972 in Tripoli.[43] In 1974 the Faculties of Science, Engineering, and Dentistry were founded in Benghazi and that same year the Faculty of Medicine opened in Tripoli.

The student body began to grow gradually. Between 1958 and 1964 the increase was less than 200 students per year or a declining proportion of the total high school population in Libya which was increasing at a much faster rate. Between 1964 and 1968 the total number of students increased by an average of 300 students per year. The rate of increase in enrollment in terms of the total student body in the decade between 1957-58 and 1967-68 dropped from 43.2 percent to 10.6 percent. It suggests that the Sanusi government may have had a deliberate policy to keep the student body small for political or other motives. From 1968-69, the last year of the monarchy, the rate of increase rose to 16 percent and then to 18 percent in the first year of the revolution, and reached 29.8 percent in the academic year 1970-71, when the Islamic University joined the Libyan University and the Faculty of Medicine was opened in Benghazi. The rate then dropped to an average of 18.7 percent increase in the student body in the last four years between 1970-71 and 1974-75.[44]

In 1974-75 foreign students also made up 15 percent of the total student body while comprising less than 6.6 percent in the last year of the monarchy. The largest increase in foreign student enrollment took place in 1970-71, when their numbers rose from 303 in the previous year to 780, or an increase of 38.8 percent. There were 49 different nationalities represented in the schools and universities of Libya during the academic year 1974-75: 22 were African, 11 Arab, and the remaining were from various parts of the world ranging from the Philippines to Iceland.[45]

Libyan graduates were also being sent abroad on scholarships to complete their studies and obtain graduate degrees in various fields. The United States had by far the greatest number of Libyan students in fields ranging from the study of the English language to petroleum engineering, agriculture, medicine, sociology, and so forth. Great Britain came next in rank, followed by Italy, France, and West Germany.[46]

An interesting comparison can be made between the two universities of Tripoli, now Al-Fateh University, and Benghazi, now Qar Yunis University (see Table 2.10). In terms of students, the older university of Benghazi is larger, with 7,872 students in 1975, while that of Tripoli had only 4,125 students. The university of Benghazi had nine faculties (Sciences, Arts, Economics and Commerce, Law, Medicine, Arabic Language and Islamic Studies, Education, Engi-

TABLE 2.10

Growth of the Student Population at the Libyan Universities
in Tripoli and Benghazi, 1955-75

Academic Year	Libyan Students			Non-Libyan Students			Total Number of Students		
	Male	Female	Total	Male	Female	Total	Male	Female	Total
1955-56	31	0	31	0	0	0	31	0	31
1956-57	79	0	79	0	0	0	79	0	79
1957-58	181	1	182	8	4	12	189	5	194
1958-59	318	6	324	13	5	18	331	11	342
1959-60	495	12	507	31	8	39	526	20	546
1960-61	660	18	678	45	6	51	705	24	729
1961-62	857	30	887	46	9	55	913	39	942
1962-63	1,012	54	1,066	35	11	46	1,047	65	1,112
1963-64	1,127	56	1,183	69	28	97	1,196	84	1,280
1964-65	1,357	84	1,441	79	41	120	1,436	125	1,561
1965-66	1,647	140	1,787	75	29	104	1,722	169	1,891
1966-67	1,982	174	2,156	59	39	98	2,041	213	2,254
1967-68	2,157	219	2,386	88	57	146	2,245	277	2,522
1968-69	2,551	251	2,802	120	79	199	2,671	330	3,001
1969-70	3,066	294	3,360	187	116	303	3,253	410	3,663
1970-71	4,056	386	4,442	605	175	780	4,661	561	5,222
1971-72	4,811	496	5,307	745	239	984	5,556	735	6,291
1972-73	6,219	719	6,938	910	372	1,282	7,129	1,091	8,220
1973-74	7,203	888	8,091	1,011	488	1,499	8,214	1,376	9,590
1974-75	8,909	1,282	10,191	1,196	610	1,806	10,105	1,892	11,997

Source: Libyan Arab Republic, Ihsa 'at al-Ta'lim fi al-Jumhuriya
al-'Arabiya al Libiya 'an al-'Am al-Dirasi 1394-1395 AH, 1974-1975 AD
(Tripoli: Government Press, n.d.), p. 259.

neering, and Dentistry) while the university at Tripoli had only six
faculties (Sciences, Agriculture, Engineering, Education, Petroleum
Engineering and Mineralogy, and Medicine).

In terms of teaching staff, the difference between the two universities was reversed to some extent. There appeared to be more
professors at the University of Tripoli than at Benghazi. According
to the figures,[47] there were 503 faculty members at Al-Fateh University, including graduate assistants,[48] but only 477 faculty members at the University of Qar Yunis, including 91 members who were
absent on leave, studying abroad, or on official missions in other
countries. Removing graduate assistants from the total number on
the faculty staffs of the two universities, the difference between the
two in terms of faculty members would be even more striking. There
were 110 Libyan faculty members[49] and 340 non-Libyan faculty members[50] who held ranks from full professor to assistant lecturer at

the University of Tripoli in 1974-75 while at the University of Benghazi there were 181 non-Libyans and 60 Libyans who held the same ranks[51] that year as well as 145 graduate assistants.

In other words, although the University of Benghazi is older and more well-established than the one in Tripoli and has a much larger student body, the trend seems to be a movement toward Trippoli, symbolized by the more important faculty positions and larger size of the faculty there. It is perhaps a sign of things to come that in the next decade or so the university of Tripoli will emerge as the dominant one of the two. This would appear logical in view of the fact that Greater Tripoli's population is more than twice the population of the Greater Region (or muhafadha) of Benghazi and Tripoli itself is the most important urban center in Libya.

ILLITERACY

The educational program aimed at eliminating illiteracy in Libya started before the revolution under the Sanusi monarchy. From 1970 onward it received a greater impetus from the government than it had previously. That year 12 classes were started in various factories and organizations to combat functional illiteracy in those places. A program on television entitled "Barnamaj Nahw al-Nur" was begun with the aim of teaching reading and arithmetic to its audience.[52] Evening classes for adults were started as well as a special program to educate women under the auspices of a regional section of the Arab Organization for Education, Science and Culture located in Tripoli.[53] Between 1972 and 1973 the program to combat illiteracy spread from the main centers in the country to the various muhafadhat in Libya at the level of both regular classes and voluntary campaigns. In 1973 two new series of books on reading and arithmetic were published and distributed to the various provinces. Although much has been done in this area, there is still a long way to go before illiteracy is completely wiped out.

Table 2.11 shows some very interesting features concerning the regional distribution of illiteracy in Libya. The first assumption that could be made about illiteracy is the unequal distribution between rural and urban areas. This is partially substantiated by the figures. Tripoli, Benghazi, and Darna, the three muhafadhat that have more than 50 percent of their population classified in the census as urban, are also the three regions whose total illiterate population is lower than the national average of 51 percent. The difference in some cases between a rural and an urban region can be as high as 20 percent (as that between Khums and Tripoli, for instance), although it could be as narrow as 5 percent (as between Darna and Jabal al-Akhdar).

TABLE 2.11

Libyan Population Age 10 Years and Over
Who Are Illiterate in 1973
(by region and sex)

Muhafadha	Males	Females	Total Illiterate Population	Total Population over Age 10
Darna	9,761	21,828	31,589	67,147
Jabal al-Akhdar	11,586	25,949	37,805	72,278
Benghazi	23,972	49,469	73,441	167,221
Al-Khalij	14,118	25,127	39,245	60,351
Misrata	19,566	45,019	64,585	106,892
Khums	21,377	42,544	63,921	99,343
Tripoli	49,570	114,571	164,141	383,743
Zawia	27,172	50,984	78,156	143,920
Gharyan	17,305	37,789	55,094	97,093
Sabha	8,525	25,334	33,859	62,087
Total	203,222	438,614	641,836	1,260,075

Source: SPLAJ, Secretariat of Planning, Census and Statistics Department, Population Census Summary Data 1393 AH, 1973 AD (Tripoli: Government Press, n.d.), Table 17, p. 17, and Table 3, p. 3.

However, the difference in illiteracy between rural and urban populations is only true of the male population. Interestingly enough, there is absolutely no difference in the rate of illiteracy among women living in rural areas and women living in urban areas. In fact, Tripoli, with a 95.7 percent urban population according to the Census of 1973, [54] has an illiterate female population of 69.8 percent, while Misrata, with only a 14.4 percent urban population, has a 69.7 percent illiterate female population! [55]

Some possible explanations for this phenomenon have been dismissed. One such explanation is that the high illiteracy rate for women in the city is caused by the high rural migration mainly because a higher number of men migrate to the cities than women, and yet the total rate of illiteracy for men as a whole is lower in the city than in the rural areas. Another explanation is that there are more schools relative to the number of students in Misrata, for instance,

than there are in Tripoli, and consequently more opportunity for
learning. Although this is true, and there is an average of 206 students per school in Misrata while there are roughly 500 students per
school in Tripoli, [56] this average is true for men as well as for
women so it cannot be a significant factor. We were therefore
obliged to resort to the cultural dimension of the problem, and sug-
gest that families are as conservative in the cities as they are in the
rural areas about sending their daughters to school, although they
tend to be more supportive of—or perhaps less economically dependent on—their male children (for assistance in agricultural activities,
for instance) in the urban areas than in the rural areas and so send
their sons more frequently to school in the city. Urban occupations
also demand more formal education than do rural occupations, and
so preparing their sons for work in the city means sending them to
school earlier and for a longer period of time for urban parents.
However, as was pointed out earlier, this trend is changing for
women too, and under the age of 10 more girls in urban areas are
attending school than they are in rural areas. This may be due to
the fact that changes in values are taking place at a faster rate in
the city than they are in the country because of the unequal development taking place in the country as a whole.

SOME PROBLEMS WITH EDUCATIONAL DEVELOPMENT IN LIBYA

Education is considered one of the most valued assets by most
Libyans today. [57] Not only does it open doors to better jobs and higher
pay, but it brings status and prestige, limited before to those who
belonged to certain important families or tribes. There is no doubt
that the government since 1969 has responded to this need for education and made giant steps in developing the educational system. All
regions now in the country are served by at least primary schools,
and most have also intermediate and secondary schools as well. The
proportion of school children between the ages of 6 and 11 attending
primary school reached 93 percent in 1973, which makes one foresee
the end of illiteracy in the country in the near future. More schools
and classrooms are being built everyday, and new faculties have
opened their doors to university students in Tripoli and Benghazi.
However, there still remain unresolved problems, some of a general
nature, others in specific areas.
   The need to build so much in order to educate so many creates
the classical dilemma of quality education versus "quantity" education.
This is a problem that all countries in the world, both industrialized
and developing, have had to face to a different degree in the twentieth

century. For Libya it may be a matter of priority for quantity to come before quality at the early stages of the development of the educational system, with the emphasis shifting to quality at a later stage. Or quality and quantity could be developed together (a Herculean task that no nation has completely achieved), and each could slow the other down. Or finally, quality taking first place in planning could inevitably lead to an elitist system of education, as witnessed in some West European countries. Libya will have to face this basic problem very soon; each choice has its drawback and the remaining conflict is one with political, social, and economic undertones.

Another problem of perhaps more limited dimension is the dilemma faced by most Arab students in the Middle East today of vocational versus academic training.[58] It is no secret that there is undoubtedly a bias in the school and the university curricula of Libya as well as in those of other Arab countries toward an academic rather than a practical education.[59] This may be due to several factors. One may be that the curricula may reflect the attitude of most Middle Easterners toward manual work as "menial" and work done behind a desk as more prestigious. Another reason may be the fact that the Libyan educational system has been strongly influenced by the Egyptian system, which was, in part at least, molded on the French and British school and university models at a time when those emphasized "theory" to a much greater extent than their American counterparts. It would appear to us that if the Libyan educational system included some vocational training, or at least some practical training at the intermediate and secondary levels, as course requirements for all students to take as part and parcel of their overall education, this problem could to some extent be overcome.[60]

Intalconsult, the Italian consulting firm that made a massive survey of Libya, suggested giving moral and material incentives to students to enroll in technical schools and to encourage banks, factories, and other organizations who needed skilled personnel to offer training for prospective employees in their organizations (this is being done in some of the factories, for instance).[61]

The physical setup of schools is also a major problem facing the Libyan government. In order to meet the needs of a very young population it is building schools everywhere and in great numbers. However, it is not able to keep up the pace with the increase in enrollment every year. So far the government has concentrated on the development of primary schools, the level at which there is the greater demand. However, according to Italconsult, "It is hard to see how the goals of compulsory preparatory (intermediary) school reform will be met and enough young Libyans adequately trained for the 1980-1990 period unless preparatory and also secondary classroom construction is accelerated."[62] Al-Khalij, Calanscio, and the Sabha regions are in greatest need of intermediate and secondary schools.

The location of schools has been another problem. Libya has a very large territory and a small population, and consequently in order to reach all communities, schools have had to be built sometimes in very remote areas. In terms of primary schools this has been done and in itself it is a major achievement. However, intermediate schools have not yet been able to reach many areas, and most secondary schools are to be found in or around the largest cities, namely, Tripoli and Benghazi. This obliges families who live outside those areas to send their children as boarders to the city schools.[63] The difficulty in reaching secondary schools may be a major deterrent to school attendance, and a major cause for the relatively low school enrollment at that level. The building of more intermediate and secondary schools in all those areas is a high priority in government planning programs but not always feasible. A halfway solution would be to provide first-rate bus transportation to and from existing schools reaching areas at 150 kilometers maximum distance from the school, thus enabling students to attend school and yet remain home. A network of roads, however, must be built first before such a solution becomes practicable.

Planners of school and other educational facilities face yet another problem: the standard or quality of school buildings and classrooms. Although on the national level there is an adequate student/classroom ratio (an average of 30 students per classroom), this distribution is uneven in the country. Italconsult found that some regions like Gharyan, Jabal al-Akhdar, and Tubruq had substandard schools and in general evaluated 30 percent of all classrooms in Libya to be substandard.[64] This could mean anything from overcrowding (30 pupils in a room that should normally contain no more than 10) to physical need of repair to unhygienic conditions. Other school facilities such as libraries, adequate recreational grounds, school laboratories, and so forth are also lacking in a large number of schools.

In Libya, unlike many other developing countries, there is no shortage of funds to build the needed schools in the country, and therefore it is only a matter of time before many of the above-mentioned problems in the physical structure of the school system can be overcome. The shortage of manual labor in Libya has delayed the process to some extent.

There are problems of a more specific nature in the educational system of Libya. It was our original assumption that, as in many developing countries, one of the main problems in the school system would be the large number of students per teacher in the classroom. This assumption proved to be mistaken. On the national level the ratio is 23 students per teacher at the primary stage, 14.6 at the intermediate stage, and 9.3 students per teacher at the secondary school level.

When we broke down these figures at the regional level, we found out that the same proportion held true in rural as well as in urban areas, with a slightly larger number of students per teacher in the urban areas. [65] However, in this area (i.e., of teachers), there were other difficulties: first, although at the primary level of schooling there were roughly twice as many Libyan teachers as non-Libyan in 1975, at the intermediate level there were as many Libyan as non-Libyan teachers, and the the secondary level that year Libyans constituted only 15.25 percent of the total number of secondary school teachers. [66] It is important for Libyan children to be exposed to non-Libyan teachers with different backgrounds, however, the bulk of the teaching should be done by Libyan teachers. This not only makes for more consistency in teaching the school programs (by not having other educational experiences interfering with it) but also for better student/teacher/parent relationships, where cultural norms and affinities make for better communication between those of a similar background. The problem of course does not lie in Libyans being unwilling to enter the teaching profession but rather in the unavailability at the present of enough trained Libyan teachers to meet the ever-growing need for educators in Libya. Not unrelated to this is the scarcity of highly trained teachers competent enough to teach students the specialized and demanding programs of the secondary schools, especially in the science sections. As the school curriculum is continuously being revised to improve it, many teachers themselves need some in-service training to catch up with the changes and prepare themselves to teach the students. [67] Again, time is an important factor in meeting the challenge of a more complex school curriculum.

At the university level we find some of the above-mentioned problems recurring too. For instance, there were 340 non-Libyan members on the teaching staff of Al-Fateh University in Tripoli in 1975 and only 110 Libyan members. [68] At Qar Yunis University in Benghazi there were 181 non-Libyan faculty members and only 60 Libyans on the teaching staff. [69] In terms of rank, a similar distribution to that existing in the school system is to be found at university level. During the academic year 1974-75 there were no Libyans holding the rank of full professor at either university while there were 40 non-Libyan full professors at Qar Yunis and 59 at Al-Fateh. [70] In a few years' time the situation will probably be reversed as a greater number of Libyan students every year are obtaining doctorates from universities all over the world and returning home to teach.

There is also a growing concern among educators in Libya about the increasing rate of dropouts at the various levels of the school system. There are those who drop out after finishing primary school whether they graduate or fail to pass their exams. [71] Some drop out at any level if they fail rather than repeat their class and there are those who drop out during the year for no apparent reason.[72]

The enrollment at each level of the educational system is much lower than at the previous one and gives the educational structure a pyramidlike shape, with few at the top. Although education is free at all levels, and students are even paid a small monthly allowance at a university and given scholarships to do graduate work abroad, there is still this anxiety to commit oneself for so many years to nonproductive work, with young men feeling they have a responsibility toward their family to get jobs and act as providers at an early stage.

Although very impressive steps have been made in the education of women, it still remains an area where a great deal more must be achieved. Women at the secondary level represented only 11.6 percent of women at the intermediary level while the total number of men at the secondary level represented 18 percent of the total number of men at the intermediate level. In other words, not only are women fewer than men in absolute number at all levels of the education ladder, but their rate of withdrawal from schools is much higher than that of men as well. This is not due to any lack of interest on the government's part in the education of women, but rather reflects the changing but still conservative attitude of the society toward women. However, with more men and women getting an education, they as enlightened couples will expect their children to study and work as well. The same holds true for the high rate of illiteracy among women, which will probably decline very sharply in the next decade or so, especially among the younger generation.

Finally, there may be yet another problem interfering with the special abilities and interests of some students. According to some sources, the Libyan father "often imposes his will on his children and decides for them the vocation they should pursue. This is often done with a disregard for the youngsters' potentialities and interests."[73] This may lead, especially at the secondary and university levels, to more failures and a higher rate of dropouts than in a situation where students are allowed to choose their field of specialization independently. However, with high school and university graduates growing in the Libyan society and having families of their own, perhaps a greater number of them will be aware of the dangers of authoritarian father-children relationships and opt for more open relationships with their children, allowing them greater choice in defining their own future.

NOTES

1. Libyan Arab Republic (LAR), Ministry of Culture and Education, Directorate of Planning, Dirasa Tarikhiya 'an Tatawwur al-

Ta'lim fi al-Jumhuriya al-'Arabiya al-Libiya min 'Ahd al-'Uthmani ila Waqtina 1394 AH, 1974 AD (n.p., n.d.), p. 7.

2. Ibid.

3. Rif'at Ghanami al-Shaykh, Tatawwur al-Ta'lim fi Libya fi al-'Usur al-Haditha (Benghazi: Dar al-Tanmiya lil-Nashr wal-Tawzi', 1972), p. 97.

4. Ibid.

5. Ibid., pp. 113-14.

6. Dirasa Tarikhiya, p. 7.

7. For a full account of the movement, see E. E. Evans-Pritchard, The Sanusi of Cyrenaica (Oxford: Clarendon Press, 1949).

8. Al-Shaykh, p. 102.

9. Dirasa Tarikhiya, p. 8.

10. Mahmud Naji, Kitab Tarablus al-Gharb, translated from Turkish to Arabic by 'Abd al-Salam Adham and Muhammad al-Usta (Beirut: Matba'a al-Ghurayib, n.d.), p. 182.

11. Dirasa Tarikhiya, p. 8.

12. Al-Shaykh, p. 78.

13. Ibid., pp. 116-17.

14. Ibid., pp. 113-14.

15. A. J. Steele-Greig, A Short History of Education in Tripolitania (Tripolitania: Department of Education, 1947), Appendix 6, p. 35.

16. Ibid., Appendix 10, p. 39.

17. A. J. Steele-Greig, History of Education in Tripolitania (Tripolitania: Government Press, 1948), p. 33.

18. Steele-Greig, A Short History, p. 9.

19. Steele-Greig, History of Education, p. 50.

20. Ibid., p. 37.

21. Ibid., p. 38.

22. Ibid., p. 41.

23. Quote from Lord Renell of Rodd, British Military Administration of Occupied Territories in Africa During the Years 1941-1947 (London, 1948), p. 288, in Majid Khadduri, Modern Libya a Study in Political Development (Baltimore: Johns Hopkins University Press, 1963), p. 49, n. 35.

24. R. L. Le Tourneau, "Libyan Education and Its Development," in UNESCO, Report of the Mission to Libya (Frankfurt: Johannes Weisbecker, 1952), p. 20.

25. Ibid., p. 25.

26. Ibid.

27. Ibid., Appendix II, p. 57.

28. Ibid., Appendix IV, p. 58.

29. Henri Habib, Politics and Government of Revolutionary Libya (Ottawa: Le Cercle du Livre de France, 1975), p. 282.

30. Text from the Constitution of Libya, promulgated in 1951, quoted in Khadduri, Appendix III, p. 344.

31. The Libyan University, Dalil al-Jami'a al-Libiya 1971-1972 (n.p., 1972), p. 17.

32. Ibid.

33. Kingdom of Libya, Ministry of National Economy, Census and Statistical Department, Statistical Abstract 1964 (Tripoli, 1964), Table 4, p. 218.

34. Ahmed Ashiurakis, About Libya (Tripoli: Dar al-Farjani, 1973), p. 54.

35. LAR, Ministry of Planning, Census and Statistics Department, Al-Majmu'a al-Ihsa'iya 1391 AH, 1971 AD (Tripoli, 1973), Table 4, p. 96.

36. Omar I. el-Fathaly, "The Prospects of Public Political Participation in Libyan Local Government" (Ph.D. diss., Department of Government, Florida State University, 1975), p. 60.

37. LAR, Ministry of Culture and Education, Department of Planning and Development, Ihsa'at al-Ta'lim fi al-Jumhuriya al-'Arabiya al-Libiya' an al-'Am al-Dirasi 1394-1395 AH, 1974-1975 AD (Tripoli: Government Press, n.d.), pp. 6-8.

38. Ibid., p. 191.

39. Ibid., p. 192.

40. Ibid., p. 207.

41. There were 9,253 boys and 6,050 girls enrolled in primary religious and Koranic schools in 1974-75, Ihsa'at al-Ta'lim, p. 189.

42. There were only 664 students at the intermediate level in 1974-75.

43. Dalil al-Jami'a al-Libiya, pp. 17-18.

44. Our calculations.

45. Ihsa'at al-Ta'lim, pp. 12-13.

46. Ibid., p. 278.

47. There are inconsistencies in the figures for faculty members at the university of Tripoli. See Ministry of Planning and Scientific Research, Census and Statistics Department, Al-Majmu'a al-Ihsa'iya 1394 AH, 1974 AD (Tripoli, 1976), p. 104 and compare with Ihsa'at al-Ta'lim, pp. 271-73.

48. Al-Majmu'a al-Ihsa'iya, 1974, p. 104.

49. Ihsa'at al-Ta'lim, p. 271.

50. Ibid., pp. 272, 273.

51. Ibid., p. 265.

52. LAR, Ministry of Culture and Education, Taqrir 'an A'mal Wizarat al-Ta'lim wal-Tarbiya wa Aham Injazatiha fi al-Sanawat ma ba'd al-Thawra (Tripoli, 1974), p. 46.

53. Ibid., p. 49.

54. We disagree with this figure, see Chapter I. The correct figure is closer to 86.6 percent.

55. Al-Majmu'a al-Ihsa'iya, 1974, Table 18, p. 120, and Table 19, p. 121.

56. Our calculations.

57. Mustafa O. Attir, "Attitudes Towards Modernization in Libya," pilot study, University Center for Urban Research, University of Pittsburgh, July 1977, Appendix C, Tables 7 and 8.

58. See el-Fathally, "The Prospects of Public Political Participation," p. 60; see also LAR, Ministry of Culture and Education, Taqrir 'an Qita' al-Ta'lim wal-Tarbiya min 68/69 ila 1975 (pamphlet, n.d., n.p.), p. 6.

59. This appears to be true of most Latin American countries as well. Paulston describes it as "a theoretical education aimed at liberating the few it can reach from the prosaic endeavours of earning a livelihood." Rolland G. Paulston, Society, Schools and Progress in Peru (New York: Pergamon Press, 1971), p. 218.

60. The courses could be varied in order to appeal to the students and should offer some choice, such as practical training in carpentry, electrical installation, car repair, plumbing, and so forth.

61. Italconsult for the Libyan Arab Republic, Ministry of Planning and Scientific Research, Settlement Pattern Study, National Report (Rome, 1976), p. 151.

62. Ibid., pp. xiv-xv.

63. Ibid., p. 203.

64. Ibid., p. 204.

65. Our calculations were based on two tables in Ihsa' at al-Ta'lim, pp. 18, 25.

66. Ibid., p. 26.

67. Taqrir 'an A'mal Wizarat al-Ta'lim, p. 52.

68. Ihsa' at al-Ta'lim, pp. 271, 272, not including graduate assistants or members who were sent abroad for various reasons.

69. Ibid., p. 265.

70. Ibid., pp. 265, 271, 272. The situation seems to have changed a bit since then. There were in 1978 Libyan professors having the rank of full professor on both campuses.

71. See the method set out by Nasr al-Din Mustafa al-Katib concerning the calculation of the yearly rate of dropouts, "Al-Ihdar al-Tarbawi," in Socialist People's Libyan Arab Jamahiriya (SPLAJ), Secretariat of Education and Culture, Center for Documentation and Research, "Al-Tawthiq wal-Buhuth al-Tarbawiya," mimeographed (n.p., n.d.), pp. 9-17.

72. Ibid.

73. Ahmed Ali al-Fenaish, "Developing an Educational Guidance Program for Libya," in University of Libya, Bulletin of the Faculty of Education 2 (1971): 5.

Chapter 3

WOMEN IN MODERN LIBYA

INTRODUCTION

Athough this chapter is concerned with the Libyan woman in the last decade—her achievements in the educational and economic spheres and some of the problems she faces today—the degree of her emancipation cannot be assessed outside the total framework of the society. It is only by understanding the kind of social and cultural milieu in which she has been living for centuries that we can then better understand how far she has gone in the last few years. It is also only by viewing the political history of the country in the last 60 years that we can begin to have some idea of why so little attention was paid to the status and rights of Libyan women until recently. Here, however, we can only give a brief sketch of the sociocultural and political background against which women's emancipation in Libya has taken place.

For centuries two worlds have coexisted in Libya (as well as in many other Middle Eastern countries), the man's world and the woman's world: each a cohesive whole, regulated by its own cultural norms, and internally structured hierarchically by various factors, such as age and lineage. The relations between those two worlds took place according to a strict code of behavior, and husbands and wives spent little time together during the day. Within each world men and women led separate lives, praying, eating, and socializing with members of their own sex only.[1] Women "belonged" to men: first, to their fathers' family, tribe, or clan and then to their husbands'. To have their own separate identity, life, or career was unthinkable. Until 1951 less than 10 percent of the adult Libyan population had ever attended school, the vast majority of Libyan women being therefore illiterate. Women were expected to be submissive to men, modest and patient, and their whole function in life was to bear children, take care of their home, and integrate into the social fabric of the extended family and the tribe.

Although from the mid-nineteenth century onward the emancipation of women in other parts of the Middle East had begun to take place, Libya remained far behind in this respect. This was due in great measure to the major political and economic upheavals that shook the country in the first half of the twentieth century, and relegated the whole issue of women to the background. In a span of less than 60 years, Libya changed from an Ottoman province to an Italian colony, was brought into World War II, and then spent seven years under a British military administration until 1951,[2] when it was eventually granted independence under a monarchy, which was overthrown and replaced by a radical socialist government in 1969. It also changed overnight, so to speak, from one of the poorest and least developed nations in the world to one of the major Arab oil-exporting countries to the West. It is against this background that women's emancipation in different spheres will be discussed.

SOME VITAL STATISTICS ABOUT LIBYAN WOMEN

The estimated mid-year population of Libya in 1976 was 2,512,000.[3] Of this it was estimated that females numbered 1,163,000 and males 1,349,000. In other words, there appeared to be roughly 1.16 males for every 1 female in Libya in 1976. The estimated proportion of males to females during the previous three years had been somewhat lower, hovering around 1.13 males for every 1 female.[4] The Vital Statistics Bulletin for 1974 gives different estimates of the population for 1973 and 1974 than the bulletins of 1975 and 1976 for those same years. And for the year 1973, the Population Census Summary gives yet another figure (not an estimate) for 1973 that varies by 33,478 from the figure given in the Vital Statistics Bulletin of 1974.[5] Thus the published figures and estimates for 1973 concerning the total population range from 2,282,700 to 2,249,222 to 2,242,000 in those three sources. However, what is important here is that the proportion of males to females for those years was the same, namely 1.13 males for every 1 female, whatever source was used, whether as a census figure or a mid-year estimate. In other words, in 1976 the number of women as compared to the number of men actually decreased relative to the three previous years, which is a rather puzzling fact.

However, it is rather difficult to know exactly the number of females in Libya because there is a consistent underreporting by

heads of households of the female members of their family. This is
a cultural tendency that is present in most Arab countries, and leads
to inaccurate figures and estimates of their populations. The International Labour Office, in conjunction with the Ministry of Work and
the Ministry of Planning in Libya, came up with a formula for the
correction of this type of inaccuracy. They took the number of individuals in each of the first four years of their life and the proportion
of males to females in each year and were able to correct the male-
female ratio for the 1964 census by using the algebraic formula:

$$3my = \frac{1}{16}(-y1 + 4y2 + 10y3 + 4y4 - y5)$$

where 3my stands for the corrected ratio. [6]

The figures for the number of live children in each year of life
(up to the age of four) were not available for 1973. The census itself
divides age-groups in the usual five-year groupings (0-4, 5-9, and
so forth), and consequently it becomes impossible to apply the above-
mentioned formula to the more recent figures now available for the
1970s. The researchers' conclusion, based on that formula, was that
the correct male to female ratio for Libya in 1964 was 1.06 males
per 1 female. [7] If that ratio were still true in 1976 (which may not be
the case), then the correct number of women would be 1,272,641 instead of 1,163,000. In other words, there could be 109,641 females
in Libya who were not counted in 1976. This has very important implications for a small population like Libya's: first, the total population estimates of Libya are lower than they should be and the population is in fact larger than is believed; second, as a large number
of women who have not been counted must be of childbearing age, the
population forecasts based on existing figures will tend to underesti-
mate the future growth of the population; third, there may be a
smaller proportion of females in schools than is believed, a higher
rate of illiteracy among females, and a smaller proportion of women
in the work force, as their percentages were based on the total female
population in Libya and that population is in fact bigger than was
thought. Apart from the mathematical ratio, it is also most probable
that females who were not reported to the census researcher are also
the ones who are not encouraged to go to school or to work outside
the home.

Another reason for the smaller number of females as compared
to males can be found in the figures concerning the deathrate of females in Libya. The birthrate and deathrate of the Libyan female
population are, in general, in accordance with those to be found elsewhere in the world. There are fewer females born than there are
males in any particular year, and there are also fewer females who
die than males in any particular year. [8] What is interesting to point

out here is that due to underreporting of females one would have expected a much lower proportion of females to be mentioned in the census under the age of one than is actually the case. One explanation would be that there may be underreporting of both male and female infants under the age of one because parents are still unsure as to whether their infant will live or die in the early months of its life. The distribution of male and female deaths by age-group is also similar to that found in the rest of the world, in the sense that in the age-groups of the five year olds and above the proportion of female deaths is lower than that of males. The fluctuation by age-group is therefore an expected one, except for two groups: that from birth to 1 year of age, and the 1 to 4 age-group, where one would expect a lower mortality of females as compared to males. The actual number of deaths in Libya is about equal for both sexes in each of these two groups.[9] The World Health Organization statistics published in 1977 give figures for most countries of the world on the distribution of child mortality by age and sex. For example, of the total number of children in 1975 between the ages of 1 and 4 who died in Canada[10] 42.4 percent were females, in the United States 43.1 percent were females,[11] in Japan 43 percent,[12] in Poland 41.8 percent,[13] in France 41.2 percent were females,[14] and in Denmark only 37.6 percent of the children between the ages of 1 and 4 who died were females.[15] Thus the female mortality rates for those countries for children between ages 1 and 4 range between 37.6 percent and 43.1 percent of the total number of deaths. In Libya the proportion reached 49 percent in 1976 and a record 52.7 percent in 1973 for females in that age-group.[16] Consequently, as there are fewer female children born than male children and roughly the same proportion die in early childhood, it is natural that there should be more males than females in Libya, even after corrections are made to account for those unreported.

Christiane Souriau, in her study of women in Libya, maintains that one of the main reasons for this unusual sex ratio may be due to the high mortality of young women due to repeated pregnancies and poor medical assistance at childbirth.[17] Although a very sound assumption, I have found no evidence to substantiate it. In looking at the vital statistics of the past few years concerning the death rate of females of childbearing age, as compared to males within that age-group, the ratio was similar to that found in other parts of the world. For instance, in 1976, women in Libya between the ages of 20 and 50 accounted for only 39.7 percent of the total death rate of the population in that age-group,[18] and those between 10 and 20 who may be supposed to have had a higher mortality rate due to very early marriages and pregnancies constituted only 36.4 percent of the total death rate in that age-group.[19] It is therefore not due to a high mortality rate during childbearing years that women constitute a smaller proportion of the society than men.

Based on the available statistical evidence it is our contention that this unusual sex ratio in Libya is primarily due to high female mortality in the first five years of life. Female children although stronger by nature than male children, die in almost equal number (until the age of 5) because in many cases they may be less well nourished than their brothers, and less often taken to the hospital or to the physician when they are sick, <u>for as females they are less valued by their family</u>. This point was brought forcefully to us when Dr. Peter L. Pellet, the well-known British nutritionist, discussed the cases of malnutrition in infants at the principal children's hospital in Tripoli in a lecture given at the Arab Development Institute in May 1978, and admitted that of the 15 undernourished infants he had seen at that hospital <u>all</u> were females!

WOMEN AND MARRIAGE

The population census of 1973 has an interesting table on the marital status of the Libyan population over 15 years of age. Of a total of 477,872 women over that age almost 72 percent were married at the time the census was taken, 3.76 percent were divorced, 11.6 percent were widowed, and 12.48 percent were unmarried.[20] Those figures are interesting sociologically when compared to the figures on the marital status of Libyan men. Out of a total of 518,883 men over the age of 15, 67 percent were married, 1.48 percent were divorced, only 1.44 percent were widowed as compared to 11.6 percent of the Libyan women, and finally almost 30 percent were unmarried.[21]

Those figures illustrate some of the problems of marriage that exist in Libya, which shall be discussed later. However, in summary we could point out some of the major issues. For instance, the much higher percentage of widows as compared to widowers may be due in part to the often large age gap between husband and wife in Libya as well as to the natural higher male mortality rate especially in the age-groups over 50. In addition, the rather high percentage of unmarried men as compared to unmarried women is probably due to several factors:

- Culturally, women marry much younger than men.
- Men postpone marriage in order to continue their studies, find work, and so forth, while women rarely do.
- The law permits women to marry at 16 A.H. (age $15\frac{1}{2}$) while the legal age for men is 18 A.H.

- Culturally, it is acceptable to be an unmarried man while it is almost shameful for a woman to remain unmarried, hence women are under greater pressure than men to get married.
- Men often have to support parents, younger brothers or sisters, orphaned nephews and nieces, and consequently hesitate to assume the burden of a family of their own.
- Perhaps the most important deterrent to Libyan men to marry early is the <u>mahr</u>, or male dowry, that the future bridegroom has to pay for his bride. The sum is often so prohibitive that young men can simply not afford to get married.

Although there is no table (to my knowledge) concerning the preferential ages of marriage of men to women in Libya, a fair idea of the age difference most frequent among Libyan couples can be obtained from a table on the distribution of births in a given year, by sex and age-groups of parents. The largest number of births for three consecutive years 1972-74, inclusive, occurred to fathers between the ages of 25 and 40, and mothers in their twenties. For those age-groups that had the highest birthrate in each of the given years, the age difference between the husbands and the wives ranged between 10 and 15 years.[22] Although this is not the most accurate way of measuring the preferential age gap between married couples, I believe this to be a fair estimate of the average age difference between wives and husbands in Libya. Nonetheless, there is in Libya, as anywhere else in the world, the whole range and gamut of age combinations between men and women, from women 45 and over married to men 20 years their junior (and getting children),[23] to men 60 years and over married to women under the age of 20 (and getting children).[24]

In general however, the age difference is greater than in Western countries and one of the main reasons for this may be the social custom in Libya of the prohibitive dowry (mahr) a man has to pay in order to get married. The mahr today goes up to 3,000 and 4,000 Libyan dinars (around US$10,000) in cities like Tripoli and Benghazi. Over and above this sum are included the gifts that the husband-to-be must offer this bride during the marriage week, such as clothes, jewels, perfumes, and so forth.[25] Those gifts are called <u>al-biyan</u> in Libya. Very often the marriage contract also stipulates that the bridegroom should provide his bride with an independent house from that of his family's and that he should have it completely furnished (the value of the furniture being set a priori in the contract).[26] The mahr as well as all the other financial clauses of the marriage contract mentioned above are both an advantage and a disadvantage to the woman. They are an advantage in the sense that the dowry is hers alone, and ensures that she obtains all she needs in her wedding "trousseau" without burdening her family with the expenses. The gifts, particularly those of gold and jewels, are also an insurance to her so that if she ever needed money at any time during her marriage she would be able to dispose of her jewels as she chose. The clauses that include the house and furniture are also a safeguard in the sense that she need not live with her in-laws but could have a house all ready to move in as soon as she was married. [27]

There are several disadvantages in this system. First, all those expenses may prove a deterrent to young suitors of a more suitable age and leave the door open to older men who could better afford all that a marriage contract required. This would of course lead to a big age gap between the spouses. Second, the husband may have borrowed money in order to cover all those expenses and consequently the couple would start their marital life already deeply in debt. Third, more and more young men not wishing to remain bachelors yet at the same time unable to afford marrying a Libyan girl frequently resort to marrying non-Libyan females, while Libyan females rarely have the same option. [28] Of course the major protection that the woman has is based on the Islamic marriage law concerning the muqadama* and the mu'akhkhara. The mu'akhkhara is the agreed upon sum of money that is set apart in the contract in case of divorce and that the husband must pay the woman to compensate her for having been divorced. The mu'akhkhara, like the mahr, is an economic deterrent to men to divorce their wives too easily, as the financial loss would then be substantial.

MARRIAGE CUSTOMS IN LIBYA

As in other parts of the Arab world marriage customs vary from region to region within the country, and are affected by the social and economic environment in which the marriage takes place. The harshest customs are perhaps those found in urban centers, where a young woman is given little or no say at all in the choice of her life partner and where she often sees her husband for the first time on the night of their wedding. Those who make all the decisions for her are usually her mother, father, uncles, and aunts. Other relatives and professional matchmakers may also be involved in the

---

*The muqadama is the bride price which the bridegroom or his father pays to the wife when the marriage contract is signed. See Monroe Berger, The Arab World Today (Garden City, N.Y.: Doubleday, 1962), p. 106.

process.[29] However, this custom is changing rapidly in the cities, mainly because of the influence of education on both women and men.

In rural areas there seems to be more freedom only in the sense that the young people are able to see each other before getting married (naturally in the company of chaperones). However, as in the urban centers they have little choice as to whom they will eventually marry.[30]

It is perhaps among the nomads, the bedouins, that we find the greatest freedom of choice. Because of their way of life it becomes almost impossible for women to be kept apart and in seclusion. Souriau quotes a Libyan journalist writing about a famous nomadic people of the region, "I have never seen people so gay and generous as the Touaregs. Love is their philosophy. The young man and young woman can show love to each other openly in front of their families. He can take her in all simplicity to sit under trees, and after putting his sword between them he will court her chastely. . . . The strange thing here is that the young woman's face is uncovered whilst the young man wears the veil (the litham). . . ."[31]

In the Fezzan, the southern region of Libya, a young man may himself go to the house of a young girl belonging to a "suitable" family, and meet her mother. If she welcomes him warmly he will then repeat his visit several times until finally the girl will appear and sit with him, chaperoned by her mother, and serve tea. It is only after he has seen her often and they have become acquainted with each other, that the young man will ask to meet the other members of the girl's family. Finally, the fathers of the young couple will meet and agree upon the conditions of the marriage contract, after which the marriage can take place.[32]

The choice of a marriage partner is made along certain lines in Libya, as in other parts of the world. Although there is no formal study as to how Libyans intermarry in the various regions of the country, a study carried out by Jamil Hilal of three main tribes in Maslata, a rural area southeast of Tripoli, provides insight into the preferential marriage patterns in the country.[33] Ironically, one fact emerging from this study is that those alliances which are traditionally the most valued by Libyan families are also the ones that occur the least frequently.[34] The most valued marriage is that between a man and his first cousin, i.e., the daughter of his father's brother. However, among the tribes he studied Hilal found that only an average of 9.6 percent of the younger generation had such a marriage (there was a great deal of variation, however, between the tribes). The second preferential choice of a spouse is one from among close relatives, and that accounted for an average of only 11.7 percent of the marriages among the younger generation of the three tribes in Maslata. Marriages from among members of the same tribe come third in preferential choice, and yet accounted for only 16.2 percent of the marriages of that generation. Marriages ranking fourth in the value hierarchy, i.e., those among young people who are not related by blood but who come from the same region, accounted for 41.1 percent of the total number of marriages. Finally, marriages which occurred between young individuals who neither came from the same family (clan or tribe) or from the same region averaged 21.2 percent.[35] Thus we may conclude that in spite of very strict customs concerning the choice of a spouse in Libya, there is in fact a great deal more freedom than one suspects. Factors such as education and migration have altered traditional marriage patterns in Libya. Education, for instance, has led women to become more aware of their rights than ever before. By going to school and especially to a university, a woman has mingled more freely with other people outside her immediate and extended family and, consequently, has found that she has more possibilities and more choices of marriage partners than those traditionally allotted to her. Migration of men from rural to urban areas, which is very high in Libya, is another factor that has led many to settle in the cities and take a wife from outside their region and unrelated to them by blood.

The marriage ceremonies and festivities, called hafalat al-zafaf, last seven days. Each day has its own name and its own customs depending on the region in Libya. On the first day, yawm al-fatiha, the marriage contract is signed, the appropriate verses from the Qur'an are read, and members of both the bride and the bridegroom's families are invited to attend. Usually, the couple is not present, but two members of their families represent them at the ceremony. On the second day, yawm al-qafa or yawm al-rami, the bridegroom's family sends gifts to the bride's family, often carried on camelback (in rural areas) in full public view, a display of wealth that enhances the prestige of the family. It usually includes perfumes, incense and myrrh, clothes, and so forth. The mothers of the bride and bridegroom receive women relatives and friends in their respective homes, and serve food and sweets throughout the day. On the third day, yawm al-henna al-saghira, the hands and feet of the bride and of all her unmarried female friends and relatives are dyed with the red henna dye. The following day, yawm al-henna al-kabira or laylat al-hajma, all the elderly and the married women friends and relatives have their hands and feet dyed with henna. On the fifth day, laylat al-dukhul, the bride is taken to the bridegroom's house riding on a camel (among the nomad and rural people), and accompanied by a great many relatives also astride on camelback. In the city the bride rides in a car all decorated with white flowers and is followed by a whole fleet of cars hooting behind her. A sheep is often killed before the bride as she steps into her new home, and water is poured

over the head of the bridegroom as he crosses the threshold of his
house. It is also customary for the bride and groom to give each
other a piece of sugar on that day. It is on the evening of the fifth
day that the marriage is consummated. Afterward the bridegroom
is taken by his men friends and relatives to another house where a
party is held in his honor with female dancers (al-sadarat) and singing.
(The Western "stag" party takes place after the marriage in Libya,
not before!) The bride in her new home is also surrounded by women
who keep her company the whole night, singing and dancing.

On the sixth day, yawm al-mahdar, the women in full regalia
gather for the last time in the house of the bridegroom to talk about
and assess the success of the festivities. The last day of traditional
ceremonies takes place a week later, on the Friday following yawm
al-mahdar, on which day (yawm al-usbu') the bride's family sends
the groom's family a cooked meal, and the bridegroom has supper
with his father for the first time since he was married, a symbolic
gesture to "renew," after a temporary break, the son's ties to his
father and his father's family and tribe. And so ends the marriage
festivities that join not just two individuals but also two families and
often two clans and two tribes as well.[36]

Polygyny is often raised as an issue in the Middle East. In
some Arab countries it may constitute a significant proportion of the
marriages, but in Libya this is not the case. The census figures of
1973 show that 96.7 percent of all families in Libya are monogamous
families; 3.2 percent of the marriages include one man having two
wives and in general two separate households; and 0.1 percent only
of the Libyan families include more than two wives.[37] Hilal, in his
study of the rural community of Maslata in the mid-1960s, found this
same proportion to be true. This low proportion therefore appears
not to be a consequence of development in education or any other
factor, but rather a kind of cultural constant. Hilal also states that
one of the reasons for polygyny in Libya seems to be the desire to
have sons. Thus even if a man is happily married and has only daughters but no sons (or only one or two), he may wish to remarry in
order to have more male children.[38] This may be due to the fact that
his first wife may have become too old to bear more children, or to
the erroneous assumption that it is the woman who determines the
sex of the unborn child and that a woman who has borne only daughters
during her first years of marriage will continue to do so. Consequently, a change of wife might mean a change in the sex of the children to come, sons being very important for a man's social prestige
as well as for the manpower they provide to assist him in agricultural
and pastoral activities.

An increase in wealth may be another reason that leads a man
to take another wife, as he can then afford two separate households
as well as the expenses for the upkeep of two separate families.

Third, according to Hilal, a man may take another wife when he has become independent from his paternal family (due to migration, education, increase in wealth, or the death of his father) because he may feel that the choice of a wife had been made for him and that he could now take a wife of his own choice. In support of this claim, Hilal points to the fact that most second marriages take place generally when a man is middle-aged.[39]

There is a new development in Libya concerning polygyny. Mu'ammar al-Qadhdhafi, at a religious symposium in the great Mosque of Mawlay Muhammad in Tripoli, on July 3, 1978, discussed with religious Muslim dignitaries from all over the Arab world the practice of polygyny (among other subjects). He insisted on the fact that the marriage of one man to more than one woman had been mentioned in only one verse of the Qur'an, and that in fact there were so many conditions preceding and following it that in only very exceptional cases was it permitted in Islam to marry more than one woman. It thus appears likely that in the very near future the state will make polygyny almost obsolete.[40]

MARRIAGE LAWS IN LIBYA

The recent legislation of the Libyan government pertaining to women's rights in marriage is determined in accordance with religious Islamic law. However, although there are Islamic laws applicable everywhere in the Muslim world that regulate marriage, divorce, and so forth (which we shall not discuss here), there are various interpretations of those laws that vary from country to country. Law No. 176, of 1972, is one such law. It stipulates that a woman may not marry before the age of 16 Muslim years (or about $15\frac{1}{2}$ years) and a man before the age of 18 Muslim years (or about $17\frac{1}{2}$ years).[41] Article 2 of that same law states that the father (or the legal guardian) may not oblige the girl to marry against her wish. Both the father (or guardian) and the daughter must give their consent for the marriage to be valid.[42] This is based on the Hanafi school of jurisprudense, and is different in some other Muslim countries, where the father's consent is not a requirement for the validity of the marriage if the girl is over a certain age. Article 3 of Law No. 176 qualifies the previous article by giving the right to a woman to bring her case to court if she feels that her father or her guardian has unfairly forbidden her to marry the man who wants to marry. If her case is convincing she may be granted permission to marry him by the court, overruling her father's objections.[43]

DIVORCE

In terms of the number of marriages and divorces per year the statistics show an interesting trend: although the total number of marriages taking place each consecutive year between 1972 and 1976 has been increasing steadily, the result in part at least of the natural increase in the population, the number of divorces has actually declined in proportion over those five years (probably due to the fact that divorce laws have become more stringent). The proportion of divorces to marriages taking place in the same year decreased from one divorce per 3.1 marriages taking place in 1972 to one divorce per 3.8 marriages taking place in 1976.[44] 'Ali al-Fenaish believes that those figures may not be very accurate as a large number of marriages and divorces that take place among the nomadic sector of the population are never officially recorded.

Some of the causes of divorce that Hilal found in his study of Maslata may be true not only of Libya as a whole but of many of the countries of the Arab world. He found that conflicting family pressures and the interference of the families-in-law in the affairs of a young couple often created tension between them, even leading in some cases to the breakup of the marriage. Another frequent cause of divorce (and perhaps the most important) appeared to be the inability of a woman to have children. A man's impotence was cause for a bride's family to ask for a divorce. There also seems to be an inverse proportion between the number of children in a family and the divorce rate in Libya.[45] Al-Fenaish, on the other hand, believes that divorce results from lack of love and communication between spouses whose marriage was arranged by their families, without any consideration for the couple's feelings for each other. In fact, a great many letters that were written by women in the mid and late 1970s to the woman's magazine al-Mar'a bear witness to the unhappiness of many young wives with their conjugal life. They often complained in their letters that their husbands had little to say to them, they were always out working or with men friends, they never showed affection to them, and so forth.[46] In many cases this lack of communication appears to be not only a result of a lack of mutual feelings of love and affection, but also due to great differences in age where a wife is often considered more a child than a woman.

Although the right of divorce (al-talaq) is a man's right in Islam, the woman also has the right to ask for divorce in some cases (this is termed al-tatliq lil-idrar). The reasons she may give are many, among them: that her husband stopped talking to her, stopped making love to her, beat her, insulted her, forced her to do sinful things, or abandoned her, and so forth.[47] The process of obtaining a divorce in this way involves the appointment of two men, one of each of the woman's family and the man's family, who are given a month to try to sort things out and reconcile the couple. If they fail and decide that the man is at fault, their verdict is given to the court, which then orders the divorce to take place, whereby the woman retains all her rights of a divorced woman (i.e., the right to marry again, her portion of the mu'akhkhara, her rights on the children for a certain number of years, alimony for them, and so forth).[48]

If she cannot prove any "bad" behavior on the part of her husband and yet is so unhappy with him that she wishes to be divorced, the woman has another way of obtaining a divorce. This method is called al-khali' or al-mukhala'a (literally, to undress), which is an agreement between both parties to divorce and does not involve the courts, although it is at the woman's request. It revolves around the transfer of money or property from the wife to the husband in exchange for the divorce.[49] Her rights concerning her children and the alimony for them remain untouched, but the mu'akhkhara may or may not be paid, depending on the written agreement she has concluded with her husband.

An addendum to those laws should be added here. Although up to now the laws concerning divorce have been in favor of the man, al-Qadhdhafi has been demanding a change of laws in such a way that women may have more rights. "Divorce," he states, "should not take place from one side only, both parties should agree to it, and it should be done before a court of justice."[50] He was referring to al-talaq whereby a man, traditionally, needed only two witnesses before whom he repeated the words "I divorce you" three times for the wife to be divorced. This change that al-Qadhdhafi has been demanding is expected to become law in the near future as it has become in many other Muslim countries.

WORKING WOMEN IN THE URBAN SECTOR

The importance of women in the development of the country has been recognized by the Libyan government. In a lecture delivered at the university in Tripoli in the early days of the Revolution, Qadhdhafi observed that "Women are half the society. They play a very important role in the life of a society . . . and in the process of revolutionary development."[51] Throughout the last decade women have been actively encouraged to take up employment outside their home. The opportunities are plentiful, and now with mandatory education for all up to the intermediate level, and available at later stages, women can freely acquire the needed skills to enter any profession they choose. The major barrier, however, is the cultural one, which is eroding slowly as more women and men are being exposed through education, the mass media, and so forth to another way of life.

Although women are encouraged to enter any profession they choose, they are not allowed by law to enter fields in which physical endurance and strength are required, such as heavy construction work, road building, employment in iron and steel factories, and so forth. [52] Instead, women have been recruited mainly in the teaching profession, nursing, clerical positions (such as secretaries), housekeeping services, and in some industries (such as the clothing and textile industries).

As can be seen in Table 3.1, of the educated and skilled working women those in the teaching profession comprise the largest group. Libyan female teachers are increasing in number every year and gradually replacing the non-Libyans (mainly Egyptians) who were hired in the 1960s when schools were being built for girls but had insufficient teaching staffs. The Libyan government passed legislation forbidding women who graduated from teachers' training colleges from working in any other field but teaching. [53] Teachers' training colleges have also limited the enrollment of male students to 1,000 and increased the enrollment of female students to 2,500 in order to train more female teachers and give them more opportunities in those fields where the government feels there is a greater need for their services. In fact, as far as could be ascertained, teaching is of a higher status than clerical work, for instance, and is more socially and culturally acceptable to families as teaching is done principally at girls' schools that have very few or no male members on their staff.

Women in the nursing and health services are rapidly increasing in number as well. Up to 1973 there were 1,969 women involved in nursing and other health services (see Table 3.1). By 1976, however, there were 22 schools for training assistant nurses and 1,897 assistant nurses had graduated that year alone, of which 209 became trained midwives after receiving a nursing certificate and 70 specialized in some form of care for the mentally ill. [54] Because of the level of education of women in Libya and in order to ensure that the hospitals have the basic help they need in order to function, the prerequisite to enter a nursing school is a primary school certificate. The training period for an assistant nurse is only 18 months. All major hospitals and clinics in Libya, however, have been obliged to hire personnel from the Arab world, Pakistan, and Europe because health care in Libya is developing very rapidly and hospitals are being built in all major towns at a faster rate than personnel can be trained. In spite of all their efforts at recruiting and training people, most hospitals and health units in Libya are still understaffed at all levels.

TABLE 3.1

Nonagricultural Occupations of Libyan Women, 1973

Occupation	Number of Women
Teaching	4,316
Nursing and health services	1,969
Administrative and clerical occupations (typists, telephone operators, government employees, and so forth)	728
Sales (owners of shops or salespeople)	133
Housekeeping services	6,546
Production workers (carpet industry, clothing industry, tobacco industry, and so forth)	2,374
Professionals and performing artists	92
Total	16,076

Source: Research Center, University of Benghazi, Lamha 'an al-Wad' al-Iqtisadi wal-Ijtima' i lil-Mar' a fi al-Jumhuriya al-'Arabiya al-Libiya (Benghazi, 1975), pp. 30-32.

Women are also actively encouraged to take up clerical and administrative jobs. There is a very serious shortage of trained secretaries in Libya, and in that field as in nursing and teaching Egyptian, Palestinian, Syria, and Jordanian women are filling those positions, albeit temporarily. However, as the figures indicate, there is a greater reluctance of families to allow their daughters to become secretaries. The free intermingling of the sexes in an office for the greater part of the day is culturally unacceptable. Yet the Women's Union in Libya has among its other activities a training center for women that includes typing in its program, over and above the usual reading, writing, sewing, and knitting programs, and according to the union's figures there were in 1978 800 women attending classes daily.[55]

There will probably be an increase in the future in the number of women working in some of the industries due in part at least to the shortage of manpower in Libya. In 1975, there were already 450 women working in one of the clothing factories of Darna that had opened the previous year.[56] During an apprenticeship a woman simultaneously learns and earns 50 dinars per month (around $150). When the apprenticeship is completed, her salary rises to 80 dinars (or about $240) per month. As in other industries transport is free to ensure a regular daily turnout. The traditional rug or "klim" manufacture is encouraged by the government, which provides the materials and also distributes and sells the rugs on the market at no profit. In factories in Darna and Misrata, Siba al-Fahoum noted that only women worked on those rugs and in Darna the director of the factory was a woman. Misrata not only produced rugs but had a training center in which women were taught how to weave them. It had also a "house-service" whereby teachers went from home to home teaching housewives to sew, supervising them, and buying their work and selling it on the market. [57]

The textile industry employs women and pays salaries equal to men's for the same work. In Benghazi the owner of one such factory stated that eventually women would replace men altogether in that industry. [58] Women are also employed in shoe factories in Darna, for instance, where they earn 30 dinars per month as apprentices and then begin earning a regular salary once they have learned their trade. Both at the shoe factory and at the textile factory hot meals and transport were provided free of charge for the workers. State-owned tobacco factories employ women. Women (only) are taught in those factories how to read and write during their working hours (two hours daily), without losing any pay. In order to encourage them to work, free meals, transport, medical services, and coffee are provided. Women are also to be found in small industries such as the match industry and in a few bakeries. [59] However, women in industry still constitute a very small (albeit growing) proportion of the women in Libya who are part of the work force.

There has been a decline in the last few years in the employment of women in housekeeping services, who according to the statistics of 1973 constituted the largest proportion of working women in Libya (in nonagricultural occupations). This is due mainly to the fact that women who wish to work have so many opportunities to do so with better pay, more regular hours, free transport, and more social prestige that they no longer need to do housekeeping chores to earn a living. In fact the domestic problem in Libya is so acute today that families who wish to employ servants go to great lengths and cost to get maids from Egypt or Tunisia.

Although the figures mentioned above (see Table 3.1) give a general idea of the trends in the employment of women, they should be used with some reservations. The most reliable data on working women probably are on women in the teaching and administrative/clerical professions. This is due to the fact that schools, offices, and government organizations can and do keep records of their employees. However, in the health services, for instance, the problem of keeping records is more difficult. In 1973, for example, there were 500 registered Libyan midwives in Libya.[60] This number is probably only a fraction of the actual number of practicing midwives in Libya. An indication of this discrepancy between registered and practicing midwives can be found in the statistics available on home and hospital deliveries. In 1973 there were 69,756 babies born in Libya who were not delivered in hospitals (only 35,465 were delivered in hospitals)[61] and most of them must have been delivered by midwives. Consequently, the proportion of 500 midwives for almost 70,000 births is a highly unlikely one, and the reality must be that a large number of midwives are in fact practicing without a license and probably with little formal education and training, although with experience. It should be pointed out also that the 500 registered midwives also practice in hospitals, and therefore the ratio of babies to registered midwives is even higher than the 70,000 mentioned above.

Housekeeping services is another very difficult category to collect exact information on. There is no agency that provides families with housekeepers and, consequently, no records of employees. Families often get maids through people they know who employ servants who in turn know of some friends, relatives, and so forth who would be willing to work. The turnover is generally high, not organized in any formal way, and consequently information on housekeeping services is unreliable in general.

Concerning production workers, statistics are probably more reliable, but there is still a category of women not employed formally in any factory or workshop but weaving baskets, rugs, and carpets in their homes (especially in rural areas, and among nomadic and seminomadic people) that are then sold on the market. The same can be said for dressmakers who work at home and have a clientele for whom they sew. In the Middle East in general the private dressmaker is still very much the one who sews most of the dresses women wear. The number of private dressmakers is very difficult to ascertain and is most certainly much higher than the 236 mentioned in the statistics,[62] which include the women who sew in factories and workshops.

Salesworkers are in a category with very indefinite boundaries. Women help their husbands sell their products and girls are used to assist their families in the shops, but both are rarely counted as regular employees.

In short, as in the case of unpaid agricultural workers, there is a large number of economically active women in nonagricultural jobs, both paid and unpaid, who do not appear in any statistics. One should therefore look at the statistics more in terms of the type of work women in Libya are involved in and the trends in the female work force rather than at absolute numbers.

Perhaps one of the major advancements made in Libya in terms of emancipating women was in laws concerning the employment of women. Article 91 of the Law on Work No. 58, which appeared in 1970, specifies that there shall be no discrimination between men and women in terms of salary if they have the same qualifications and do the same job. [63] Article 96 of that same law states that a woman may not work more than 48 hours a week, including overtime work (this is to allow time to take care of home and children). This article also specifies that women cannot work between the hours of 8 p.m. and 7 a.m., except in those occupations that are specifically designated by the Minister of Work for night work (like nursing). [64] Women are also not allowed by law to work in mines or to hold any "arduous or perilous occupation." [65]

Those provisions of the work law were then followed by special clauses for married women with children. A woman employed for more than six months can take leave of up to 50 days with half pay to include the period of delivery of her baby. If employed for more than six months, she could obtain a whole month's leave with full pay. [66] A woman could also ask for up to 60 days' sick leave with half pay if her health condition requires her to be absent beyond the term set by law for a normal delivery. Article 97 of Law No. 58 of 1970 specifies that it is the right of a working woman to breast-feed her child for 18 months after birth and, consequently, she may take two half hours or one whole hour leave from work every day to feed her child with no reduction in her salary. These clauses, incidentally, are strictly applied, as we witnessed during our stay in Libya.

Article 98 of the Law No. 58 of 1970 states that in order to encourage the working woman with young children to continue working, any establishment employing more than 50 women at a time (factories, hospitals, and so forth) should have a nursery where a woman can leave her preschool children while she is at work. In addition, an employer is not permitted to fire a woman during her leave for delivery and until the time she returns to work. Any working woman has the right to receive 3 dinars per month ($10) from the third month of pregnancy. [67] After discussing the law with a pregnant Libyan colleague she told us that one of the clauses to that law was that the woman had to go for a monthly checkup at her clinic, only after which could she receive the 3 dinars. Thus the money is an incentive to better health care for both mother and child. Unfortunately, in spite of this financial encouragement women do not go for regular checkups.

If a woman delivers her child in one of the public hospitals all expenses are paid by the state and over and above this she receives 25 dinars or around $90 cash as a bonus for the child. [68] A working woman receives a bonus of a half month's pay for every year she has worked for up to five years when she gets married and when she has her first child. If she has worked more than five years, she receives a bonus of a whole month per year when she leaves her work and gives notice six months after the delivery of her first child.[69]

Concerning old age pensions, a woman's retirement age is 55 while a man's is 60. The pension must not be less than 30 dinars or $100 a month, or more than 80 percent of her original salary at the time of retirement, or more than a total of 150 months of salaried work. Over these there are special family allowances that increase the total sum she receives. Finally, a working woman like a man has additional compensations: she must receive 60 percent of her salary during a period of six months if on sick leave;[70] and if injured at work she receives 70 percent of her salary for at least a year even while away from her job.

WORKING WOMEN IN RURAL AREAS

Females in rural areas of Libya, like in most rural areas in the world, play a very important role in the economic development of the region. However, as the majority work as members of a family group—whether as daughters or as wives—they are generally unpaid workers and, consequently, not considered "breadwinners" by menfolk. This attitude toward the female rural worker is reflected in the 1973 national census, which gives extremely low figures for females working in agricultural activities in rural areas in Libya, although the category of rural workers, in the census, includes "unpaid family workers."[71] In spite of the fact that there are over 200,000 females over the age of 10 in the rural areas of Libya,[72] the census reports that there were only 13,761[73] economically active females in the category of Agriculture, Forestry, Hunting and Fishing. These included unpaid family workers. We believe this to be a gross misrepresentation of the unpaid female work force in the rural areas. Some of the reasons for this underrepresentation can be pointed out here. First, respondents to the census questionnaires may have believed that only those who were paid for their work were to be considered economically active (whatever the census worker may have said). Second, the cultural restraint concerning women and the almost automatic underreporting of the number of females in a household would lead heads of households to ignore the work performed by their womenfolk. Third, a man's honor, very important in all Middle Eastern societies, may be another reason affecting answers because only men are supposed to be the breadwinners. Finally, there is no doubt that there has been inaccurate reporting from those who distributed the questionnaires. This becomes clear when one analyzes the regional breakdown of female rural workers who are reported in the census. In some cases the numbers form a reasonable proportion of the rural work force, as in the case of al-Zawiya, where 6,669 Libyan females were recorded working out of a total economically active rural population of 37,636, comprising 17.7 percent of that total.[74] This is in contrast, however, to the Gharyan region, where 182 females were reported working, comprising only 0.8 percent of the 21,840 persons in the rural work force of that region.[75] The inaccurate reporting for the Khalij region was even worse: only 33 women or 0.3 percent of an economically active rural population of 10,620 were reported working, of which only 7 fell into the category of "unpaid family workers."[76]

Observers of rural development in Libya have noted that:

In rural areas, women and children may work for short periods only during the seasonal peak of agricultural demand, and this work, though limited in time, is usually very significant in terms of its contribution to output. But it will escape the attention of the census-taker. Moreover, many agricultural operations, such as tending animals or processing farm products are part of the normal duties of the housewife, and are not considered as "employment" by the census—nor even for that matter, by the farmer or the housewife herself. From an economic point of view, however, these duties represent a genuine contribution to the productive effort of the community. . . .[77]

It thus becomes abundantly clear that the figures concerning economically active women in rural areas must be revised and a calculation of their number be based on another set of factors.

Age is one factor that should be used to delineate the number of women in the rural work force. Although there were 432,983 females recorded in rural areas in 1973,[78] of which 151 were non-Libyan,[79] the actual number of Libyan females over age 10 (the age at which individuals are considered as members of the work force in Libya) in rural areas was only 218,084.[80] However, of those we should subtract 29,269 rural women over the age of 60,[81] who although still active within the confines of their homes may delegate the work in the agricultural and pastoral spheres to the younger women of the household such as daughters and daughters-in-law. The total would then be 188,815 rural women between the ages of 10 and 60.

From the above number would also have to be subtracted those females aged 10 years and above who would be attending school or any other institution for at least part of the day. This would not mean that they would not be helping out on the land or at home as well, it would only mean that they would be unable to put in as much work as would those who did not attend school. Our calculations based on the census figures for every region of the country gave us a total of 104,187 rural females between the ages of 10 and 24 attending some sort of educational institution during the day.[82] Subtracting this figure from that of women between the ages of 10 and 60 leaves a total of 84,628 females in rural areas who would be between the ages of 10 and 60 and not attending school.

Another factor should be taken into consideration in order to delimit the number of economically active females in rural areas in Libya and this is the number of mentally and physically handicapped females who cannot perform as well or to the same degree as normal females. The Population Census Summary Data of 1973 gives a total of 19,534 mentally or physically handicapped females for Libya as a whole. Of these we calculated that 10,206 were above the age of 10 and below the age of 60.[83] If we assume that the mentally and physically handicapped are distributed in equal proportion between rural and urban areas (an assumption that may not always be justified), then the rural proportion would be roughly 40 percent of that figure (Libya's population, according to the census, is about 40 percent rural and 60 percent urban). In other words, there would have been in 1973 approximately 4,082 mentally and physically handicapped females in rural areas who when subtracted from the total number of rural women between the ages of 10 and 60 not attending school would give a total of 80,546 females fit to be economically active in the rural areas of Libya.

Two additional factors should be mentioned that would increase the number of rural females. The first is the actual underreporting of the number of females to census takers mentioned earlier. Applying the ILO formula to correct this inaccuracy, whereby it was found that there were in 1964 1.06 males per 1 female[84] instead of 1.13 as recorded for 1973, and using this same ratio for 1973 the total number of rural females would increase to 463,391, or an increase of 30,408 rural females.[85] If then from this number we subtracted the same proportion of females below the age of 10 and above the age of 60, those who attended school, and those who were mentally and physically handicapped—as we did from the original number of rural females—we would get 5,473 more females fit to be economically active in rural areas, and their total would then rise to 86,019.[86]

A final factor affecting the number of rural females fit to be economically active is that a large number of females who would be considered rural by other definitions for rural and urban areas were categorized as urban by the census. Many of these females are economically active in agricultural occupations (such as raising chickens, for example), and yet are not included here because the census has them under the category of urban population. To some extent at least, these women could balance in number those who fall in our category of rural females, are fit to be economically active, and for any number of reasons are not. Thus we believe that our figure of 86,019 is closer to the reality concerning the actual female rural work force, than the figure of 13,761 mentioned by the census. However, it must be kept in mind that this is merely an approximate figure and that several factors may affect the real number of economically active females in rural areas and ought to be mentioned here in order to give a more accurate picture of the situation. Perhaps the most important element is the cultural element, which may prevent women (mainly in small rural towns) from working outside the home. Second, women over age 60 will work in the households of their husbands or sons, caring for poultry, growing vegetables, and so forth. Third, females attending educational institutions in the rural areas are not exempt from working in rural activities as well, and many work six or even seven hours a day assisting their families before and after school.

Our number of 86,019 is therefore only an estimate of the real rural female work force in Libya as some of the factors mentioned above would tend to alter this figure. It is, however, a much more realistic figure, matching well the male work force in rural areas of 96,184.[87] In other words, according to those calculations, females may comprise up to 45.7 percent of the total economically active population in rural regions of Libya and 20.6 percent of the economically active Libyan population,[88] working part time, full time, seasonally, or otherwise and yet unpaid in most cases and often not even considered working by members of their own families.

Two scholars are in agreement on this issue of the rural female work force. Muhammad Rabi', an expert on agricultural development in Libya, noted from field observation that Libyan women worked as hard if not harder than men in most agricultural activities. Siba al Fahoum, who conducted a study on Libyan women, also estimates that women working in the rural sector constitute 65 percent of the total number of women of working age in Libya.[89] We are therefore obliged to conclude that women in rural areas in Libya get little credit or recognition for their work and that statistics on rural women do not give a true picture of the reality of the situation in the country but rather reflect common cultural assumptions as to the woman's place in society.

EDUCATION OF WOMEN IN LIBYA

The most significant development in the emancipation of the Libyan woman has been in the area of education. There is little doubt that the major impetus behind the education of women has been by

TABLE 3.2

Education of Women in Schools and Universities in Libya from 1969-76

School Level	1969-70		1970-71		1971-72		1972-73		1973-74		1974-75		1975-76	
	No. of Girls	Percent of Total	No. of Girls	Percent of Total	No. of Girls	Percent of Total	No. of Girls	Percent of Total	No. of Girls	Percent of Total	No. of Girls	Percent of Total	No. of Girls	Percent of Total
Primary	107,047	34.4	128,709	36.9	159,566	39.4	190,235	42.1	214,880	44.3	234,360	45.4	254,151	45.9
Intermediate	5,707	15.7	6,554	17.7	9,055	20.9	12,728	23.3	19,181	25.9	25,401	28.1	40,042	31.9
Secondary	1,071	12.9	1,258	15.2	1,574	16.7	1,990	18.2	2,475	18.4	2,951	20.1	4,034	22.2
Teachers' training	1,679	35.5	1,984	36.9	1,897	31.7	4,087	37.2	7,574	48.5	10,966	56.1	12,544	58.7
University	299	8.9	385	8.6	496	8.3	719	10.4	888	11	1,309	12.8	—	—
Total	115,803	21.4	138,505	23.0	172,588	23.4	197,158	26.2	244,998	29.6	274,986	32.5	—	—

Note: Dash indicates information not available.

Source: LAR, Ministry of Culture and Education, Taqrir 'an Qita' al-Ta'lim wal-Tarbiya min 68/69 ila 1975 (pamphlet, n.p., n.d.), p. 15; University of Benghazi, Research Center, Lamha 'an al Wadi' al-Iqtisadi wal-Ijtima'i lil-Mar'a fi al-Jumhuriya al-'Arabiya al-Libiya (Benghazi, 1975), Table 3, p. 21, Table 4, p. 22; LAR, Ministry of Culture and Education, Department of Planning and Development, Ihsa'at al-Ta'lim fi al-Jumhuriya al-'Arabiya al-Libiya 'an al-'Am al-Dirasi 1394-1395 AH, 1974-1975 AD (Tripoli: Government Press, n.d.), p. 259.

the government. Because the country has a small population and needs manpower to develop, it was realized that women could play a major role in the educational, economic, political, and social spheres of Libyan society. Educated Libyan women could be mobilized for productive work in various fields and reduce the need of the government to import foreign workers.[90]

By law women should attend school till the intermediate level, and consequently a large number of schools for women were opened all over Libya since 1969. Unfortunately, there is no way of requiring families to send their daughters to school and, therefore, there is still a large number of girls who stop going to school after the primary level.

Table 3.2 shows some very interesting trends in the education of women between 1969 and 1976. First, not only did the absolute number of women at all levels of the educational system increase substantially every academic year, but the proportion in relation to the number of men enrolled also increased. In other words, relative to their numbers, women in schools generally increased at a higher rate than did men. At the intermediate stage, the proportion of women rose by 20 percent in eight years and their absolute number increased by more than 1,100 percent during that period! The absolute number of women at the secondary stage quadrupled in those eight years, although the proportion to the total student body at this stage rose by less than 10 percent. At the teachers' training schools we find yet another trend: between 1968 and 1972 the proportion the women actually declined from 42.6 percent to 31.7 percent of the total student body, but began rising again in 1972-73, reaching a peak of 58.7 percent of the total number of enrolled students in 1976. At the university level, the trend was again somewhat different between the academic years 1968-69 and 1971-72, when the actual proportion of women to the total student body enrolled in all universities in Libya actually declined, although their absolute number almost doubled. In other words, during that period more men than women were getting into a university and their rate of increase was higher than that of women. However, from 1972-73 onward the proportion as well as the number of women began steadily increasing. It is interesting to note here that in 1978 the number of women in the College of Education at Al-Fateh University was actually higher than the number of men.[91]

Women have also been accepted in various other fields in a university. In 1974-75 there were 52 women studying law and 53 in medicine at the University of Benghazi. At the University of Tripoli that same year, 44 women were in engineering, 37 in agriculture, and 110 in the hard sciences. The majority, however, attended the Colleges of Art and Education at both universities.[92]

In the academic year 1974-75 there were 2,394 schools (primary,

TABLE 3.3

Regional Distribution of Government Schools in Libya, 1974–75: Girls' and Mixed Schools

Region	Primary		Intermediate		Secondary		Total	
	Girls'	Mixed	Girls'	Mixed	Girls'	Mixed	Girls'	Mixed
Zawia	22	191	12	40	2	5	36	236
Tripoli	22	232	26	39	5	1	53	272
Gharyan	10	181	5	27	1	2	16	210
Khums	4	235	1	7	1	3	6	245
Masrata	15	143	2	7	1	2	18	152
Al-Khalij	6	100	2	9	1	4	9	113
Benghazi	26	121	14	17	3	1	43	139
Al-Jabal al-Akhdar	7	150	5	20	2	2	14	172
Darna	11	134	3	12	2	1	16	147
Sabha	6	107	2	11	1	1	9	119
Total	129	1,594	72	189	19	22	220	1,805

Source: LAR, Ministry of Culture and Education, Ihsa'at al-Ta'lim fi al-Jumhuriya al-'Arabiya al-Libiya 'an al-'Am al-Dirasi 1394-1395 AH, 1974-1975 AD (Tripoli, n.d.), Tables on pp. 39, 67, 95.

intermediate, and secondary)[93] in Libya. Of these 220 were for females only (see Table 3.3) and 369 were for males only.[94] The majority were mixed schools, including women and men, and making up a total of 1,805 schools. Certain factors about those statistics are rather interesting and shed light on some of the problems facing the educational system in Libya today.

The first fact is that there are fewer women per school (for girls' and mixed schools) than there are men per school (for boys' and mixed schools). There were 169.5 men per school during the academic year 1974-75 while there were only 135.7 women per school during that same year.[95] Consequently, whereas boys' schools are crowded and the proportion of men is very high in mixed schools, women have a great deal of potential space to increase in number without causing any overcrowding. In other words, relatively to their numbers, females have more schools than males.

The second fact is that although at first sight it may appear to be a great achievement in a conservative society to have 75 percent of all schools teaching men and women together, a closer look at the figures will reveal that of the total number of mixed schools 88 percent are primary schools (see Table 3.3). However, one should remember that one generation ago the sexes were not mixed in schools even at that level and, therefore, although somewhat limited this is still an achievement in liberalizing strict codes of sexual segregation.

A third fact—which at first appears the most astonishing one revealed by those figures—is the regional distribution of mixed schools at the secondary level. The three largest muhafadhat in Libya according to the 1973 census, Tripoli, Benghazi, and Darna,[96] had fewer mixed secondary schools than girls' schools. In fact, Tripoli, the most important urban center in Libya, had only one mixed secondary school in 1975 while Misrata, the least urban muhafadha of Libya, had two! Can we therefore deduce that rural areas are less conservative than urban areas in terms of allowing girls to attend mixed schools? It was pointed out that in fact almost the reverse was true. Because so few women were allowed to continue their studies beyond the obligatory intermediate stage of education in rural areas, it was not economic to build separate schools and so they had to join the boys' schools if they wished to complete high school.[97] When we calculated the proportion of women to men in secondary schools by region, this explanation was borne out completely. Whereas in Benghazi women at the secondary school level constituted 43.2 percent of the total student body in 1975, in Gharyan, a very rural region in Libya, the proportion of the student body was only 3.4 percent female at the secondary school level.[98] To a varying degree the differences in proportion between urban and rural areas were the same for all regions of Libya. However, one should point out that the fact that there were so few secondary schools for women only, could in turn cause a drastic drop in the enrollment of women at that level. In other words this is a two-way process: fewer women lead to fewer schools for females only, and fewer secondary schools for females only in turn can lead to a low enrollment of girls at the secondary school level as parents who might have allowed their daughters to continue their study in an all girls' school would be very reluctant to let them attend a mixed school.

Education of women in rural areas has taken other forms. In 1974 the Libyan government opened the first Center for Rural Development in Qarbulli, 50 km from Tripoli, to train and educate women in rural areas. By 1977, there were eight such centers all over Libya, serving or having served over 560 women during that period.[99] Those centers were an offshoot of a larger program for rural development aimed primarily at men that involved training farmers in the modern methods of agriculture, the use of tractors, chemical fertilizers, pesticides, and so forth.[100] Branches were then opened to train the women of rural areas. Independent centers with programs aimed at reaching the largest possible section of the rural female population. The requirements for enrollment in the program were minimal, namely that the candidate be the daughter of a farmer; living in the rural area of the training center; at least twelve years old; and healthy, having no disease of the stomach or the intestines.[101]

The aims of the program were ambitious: to erase illiteracy among rural females; to provide modern agricultural training in growing vegetable gardens, preserving fruits and vegetables, and rearing chickens, sheep, and even cows; to develop handicrafts and train women to make homespun rugs; to give both a religious and a civic education; to teach hygiene and first aid and to teach home economics.[102] Those who succeeded in that program were then to be further trained (if they wished) in a center for advanced study in Tripoli to become teachers in turn in the rural development center where they originally studied.[103]

Women in the rural development centers are divided into three groups: those unmarried who can read and write, those unmarried who are illiterate, and married women. The latter can bring their infants with them as most centers have nurseries equipped with cots and someone to supervise the children while the mothers are being trained.

Although each group has a kind of separate classroom schedule, they are taught the same subjects for the same number of hours a week (in the Jafara region, for instance, for which we had the curriculum).[104] This includes 3 hours per week of reading and writing (whether the group was literate or illiterate), 3 hours of practical training in agriculture, and one-hour courses each week in hygiene, civics, and religion. The bulk of the training really consists of courses in home economics (15 hours a week). These include training in housekeeping, the cooking of healthy meals (with a discussion of the food value in each element), and the use of modern home appliances in cooking, freezing, preserving, and so forth.[105]

By February 1977 there were eight such centers for rural development, the majority in the Sahl al-Jafara agricultural sector.[106] There appears to have been roughly 310 women and unmarried girls who completed their training in those centers,[107] although 560 had enrolled originally, between 1975 and the early part of 1977.[108] There are also two advanced training centers for teachers to prepare girls to teach other women in their rural area of origin the curriculum mentioned above. Those advanced training centers are to be found in Benghazi and Tripoli. Only unmarried girls are accepted in those programs because they are enrolled as boarders for one academic year, with food and board paid by the government. They also receive about 15 dinars (approximately $50) for pocket money every month.[109]

The centers for rural education face certain basic problems. The major one is perhaps the reluctance of rural men to allow their wives or daughters to attend training centers. Some centers have even had to close down due to the fact that not one woman was attending.[110] The government found itself obliged to include a special clause in the landownership contracts (at the time when landless peasants were given farmland by the government) stipulating that one of the preconditions for ownership was to send their wives and daughters to those centers to be educated and trained.[111] A number of teachers had to go to the homes of farmers and attempt to convince them of the advantages they (as men) would reap if their womenfolk were properly trained and taught.[112] The Home Economics Center of ad-Hadba al-Khadra gave an exhibition of all that had been done by the women that year and invited everyone to come and see, displaying the products and citing the names of the trainees to attract new recruits and convince the men of the area that they were indeed learning something worthwhile.[113]

Another basic problem these centers face is the insufficient number of properly trained teachers to meet the needs of all rural communities. Although the schools encourage those who graduate to either specialize and become teachers or to help out and teach other women what they themselves have learned (without having to go to the advanced teachers' schools), the majority return home and work only within their own family environment. This keeps this movement for training women from growing at a more rapid pace in rural regions.

A third problem lies in the curriculum itself, which emphasizes home economics above all else. This may be a means of convincing

women, and circumventing opposition to join the centers, by not offer-
ing a program that is too untraditional. However, it is obvious that
illiterate women should be given many more hours of reading and
writing in order to master those skills. It appears also that more
emphasis should be placed on agricultural training and the rearing
of fowl, for instance, than is actually being done.

Finally, although there are nurseries in many of the centers,
there is not much taught about child-rearing practices—not merely
infant hygiene, which of course is essential, but some basics about
child psychology and the needs of children at different stages of development. This may be of great importance in preparing this coming
generation to meet the great pressures of a rapidly modernizing
society and to cope better with the new demands that will be made on
them in decades to come.

WOMEN, CRIME, AND REHABILITATION
IN LIBYA

In dealing with the problems women face in the Middle East it
is very rare to deal with crime in relationship to women. And yet
as in all other sectors of their lives, what is considered criminal
for a woman and how it is punished is culturally defined. A Libyan
woman accused of committing a crime will find herself judged by
cultural norms that may not be applicable to men and punished or
"rehabilitated" according to those norms. These may appear at first
"unjust" but they have a "cultural rationale" that gives them legitimacy. We shall examine here some of the problems female "crimi-
nals" face in Libya.

The figures published in 1978 for crimes in Libya were for the
year 1976. The breakdown by general category of crime for that year
for women in Libya (which includes non-Libyan women as well) can
be seen in Table. 3.4.

As one can note from the classification of the crimes, there
are two separate categories for murder, one of which is the killing
of an illegitimate infant to save the honor of the family. Because the
honor ('ird) of a family is so important in Arab society, the killing
of a member of the family, usually a woman who in some way (pre-
sumably sexually) has tarnished its honor is often condoned by the
society, although not by law. The alternative to killing the woman
who has violated the honor code is often to keep the matter secret
and if an infant is born to kill the illegitimate child. Although the law
recognizes the fact that this is a major crime by classifying it separately, it also recognizes the cultural pressure that was put on the
individual and/or family to do so. The only comparison that could be

TABLE 3.4

Major Crimes Committed by Women in Libya during 1976

Type of Crime	Number of Women	
	Underage	Adult
Murder	1	4
Killing of illegitimate infant to save honor	2	7
Attempted murder	0	2
Killing due to accident or negligence	2	77
Assault	0	0
Kidnapping	0	0
Counterfeiting	0	0
Narcotics	0	3
Forgery	3	5
Rape (by married/unmarried women)	3	6
Arson	2	13
Robbery	1	0
Housebreaking	7	6
Other thefts	19	55
Stealing of vehicles for temporary use	0	0
Stealing of animals	0	2

Source: Figures based on SPLAJ, Secretariat of the Interior, General Directorate for Security Affairs, Center for Research in Criminology, Taqrir 'an Halat al-Jarima 1396 AH, 1976 AD (Tripoli, n.d. [1978?]), Table 10, p. 20.

made here, where the law takes into consideration cultural values in the case of first-degree murder, is in France where a crime passionel committed by the wronged spouse is considered a lesser offense than other cases of homicide. In some cultures crimes of vendetta, or revenge, are also dealt with more leniently because the customs and culture are the main forces behind such crimes.

Another categorization of crime that has very definitely cultural overtones is the categorization of rape into those committed against (or by) married women (al-muwaqa'a) and those committed against (or by) unmarried women (hatk al-'ird). The difference again lies in the question of honor or 'ird. An unmarried woman who is raped dishonors the name of her whole family, i.e., her father's and brothers' name. Thus the crime of rape that is committed against her is not merely a violation of her own individual person but a greater crime committed against her whole family. It is the illegitimate loss of virginity that makes the crime against the unmarried woman greater than one against a married woman. A married woman, in the eyes of the society, has lost nothing, and if the crime becomes known, dishonors only her husband (and not his family), and he need only divorce her or repudiate her to save <u>his</u> honor. We thus find here again the same crime categorized differently because of cultural norms.

Due to the above reasons we believe that there must be extensive underreporting of both rape and infant killing, as in both cases families would prefer to keep the matters secret rather than let the law interfere even to their benefit in order to protect family honor.

The larger number of crimes in Libya committed by men and women are not included in Table 3.4 as they are categorized separately in the crime statistics bulletins. These include misdemeanors and petty crimes committed in public places or against public institutions. These may include anything from breaking trees and harming the environment in general (crimes against agriculture and forestry)[114] to driving dangerously and causing accidents (crimes against public security)[115] to not paying taxes or not reporting accurately incomes received from independent sources (crimes against the protection of national wealth).[116] Under similar and other categories, adult women were responsible in 1976 for 2,971 minor crimes, of which 1,855 were classified as misdemeanors against individuals for which there is no further elaboration in the criminal statistics. Underage females number 648 accused of minor crimes, more than half of which are also categorized as misdemeanors against individuals.[117]

We thus find two basic problems with the statistics on crime in Libya. First, due to cultural norms a large number of serious crimes, primarily rape and the killing of illegitimate infants, go unreported. Thus figures on both those crimes are inaccurate, and probably will remain so, as there is no sure way of finding out what people will not report. The second problem is easier to remedy. It concerns the categorization of crimes, which is so vague that it is virtually impossible to know from the tables (except for those of the major crimes) what the individuals are accused of. A new and more explicit classification of crimes based on some international set of categories should be devised in order to facilitate the study of the phenomenon of crime in Libya and enable criminologists to undertake comparative studies with other countries of the world.

REHABILITATION

The general attitude of the government toward lawbreakers in Libya has been to rehabilitate prisoners rather than to punish them. Although the Shari'a Law is the basis of the penal code in Libya, some of its punitive injunctions have never been in fact applied. This attitude can best be seen in the way women lawbreakers have been treated. Although very little statistical information is available on women's prisons, a study was made by a member of Women Organization of Benghazi, 'Aziza al-Nafs, who became an inmate of one of the women's prisons in order to understand better their problems.[118] She did make some suggestions for improving their condition and in fact many changes were introduced.

Today, for instance, illiterate women in prisons receive classes in reading and writing.[119] Members of the women's organizations in Libya visit them regularly and prepare lessons in sewing, embroidery, and knitting. Their work is then exhibited and sold, the aim being to encourage them to learn and work and prepare them to lead a productive life once they leave the prisons.[120]

In 1971 a decree was passed by the government for the formation of a rehabilitation center for women. The goal of that center bears a strong cultural stamp:". . . to offer shelter to those minors and divorced women who are exposed to deviance, in order to guide them socially, psychologically and religiously. The aim is to improve their behaviour and enable them to return to a good family life and to adjust to the society."[121]

Those to be included in that center according to the decree were: minors who had been raped, minors who had been seduced, women accused of prostitution, women abandoned by their families because they had borne an illegitimate child, divorced women who have no source of protection or financial support, and divorced women abandoned by their family and exposed to deviant behavior.[122] In 1974 women falling under some other categories were also taken into that center: women who had been "kidnapped with the purpose of being married" (eloped?)[123] as well as those accused of stealing, vagabond women, and any woman abandoned by husband or parents with no home or source of income.

Table 3.5 shows the state of that rehabilitation center by the end of 1975. It has opened approximately three years earlier in Tripoli and was the first of its kind in Libya. Since then another center opened in Benghazi in 1976[124] and a third one in Tripoli in 1977.[125] From Table 3.5 we can note that the Arab character of the culture in which the women live determined in great part the definition of the cases accepted by the rehabilitation center. At first sight there appear to be some contradictions in the definition of who should be in the

TABLE 3.5

Type and Number of Cases in the Social Center for the Protection
of Women in Tripoli, 1975

	Number of Cases		
Type of Case	Sheltered during 1975	Left during 1975	Remaining at Year-end
Illegitimate pregnancy	56	43	33
Assaulted	27	13	24
Raped	46	38	11
Prostitute	14	12	5
Kidnapped to marry	10	7	3
Divorced with no support	11	7	7
Vagabond	9	6	3
Thief	2	2	0
Other	38	32	13
Total	213	160	99

Source: SPLAJ, Secretariat for Social Affairs and Social
Security, Dalil al-Ihsa'at al-Ijtima'iya 1395 AH, 1975 AD (n.p.,
n.d.), Vol. II, Table 94, p. 132.

center: women who have been raped or assaulted are treated in the
same way as those who are categorized as prostitutes. Women who
are divorced or abandoned by their family are included with those
who are accused of theft or vagabondage. In other words, there seems
to be no difference between the lawbreakers and the victims. However,
if one were to use the rationale of the culture the differences would
then appear minor or even disappear: an unmarried woman who
loses her virginity dishonors her family and is considered by the
society a "fallen" woman. Whether she was seduced or raped, whether
she was responsible or not, becomes an almost irrelevant issue in a
society where a woman has no separate identity of her own but "belongs" to a family, clan, or tribe. Women are then liable to be
abandoned by their family for no fault of their own, and being considered a kind of "pariah" in the society, eventually turn to prostitution as the only means of livelihood. It thus becomes very logical
and humane to shelter such women and help them to readjust to
society, and prevent them from resorting to prostitution. In the same
way prostitutes must learn not only to readjust to society but must be

given an alternative to earning a living by learning a new trade. The same logic holds for divorced women: in case of divorce it is usually the woman who is blamed and is shamed by it, rarely the man. Although most parents in the Arab world and in Libya will take their daughters back and will try to find them another husband, they may not if, for instance, they are too old, do not have the means, and so forth. Thus a divorced woman who is abandoned by her husband and by her parents and has no skill to work and nowhere to go may again be liable to resort to prostitution in order to earn a living.

We thus find that what at first appeared to be an irrational categorization of victims and lawbreakers is a rational and logical way of dealing with a real social situation, and is in fact one of the most immediate ways of assisting women who have no place to go. (The category of "thieves" probably applies to very young women, underage, whom it was found preferable to rehabilitate rather than imprison.)

However, how effective the center is in actually rehabilitating those women or in providing them with more than just a temporary shelter is another question. If one looks at certain aspects of the center there are major questions to be raised. For instance, in 1975, with 99 women to be rehabilitated at the same time (213 women came to the center at one time or another that year), [126] there were only 16 employees in the center: the director, two social workers, seven supervisors, one treasurer, and four maids. [127] Twelve of the sixteen administrative members had no educational degree (either school or university). [128] There were also no physicians, nurses, or psychiatrists. The program of the center was similar to that in other centers for training and educating Libyan women in rural and urban areas, namely, a program where all 99 women were taught to sew, knit, and embroider as well as to cook, clean, and so forth. Although those types of skills could prove useful to the women when they left the center and tried to adjust to life in society, it is by no means sufficient as a program to assist and rehabilitate women who have been assaulted, raped, or abandoned. Of the 259 women who were present at the center at one time or another during the year 1975, 77 or almost one-third stayed there less than one month and 51 stayed one month only. [129] In other words, 46.7 percent of the women stayed one month or less at that center. This is certainly not enough for any form of rehabilitation program to be of any utility whatsoever. There should be a minimum residence period of three months at the very least, in which those women could rest and sort out their problems before returning to society. Finally, another major problem that the women face is their destination after leaving the center. Of the 160 women who left the center during the year, more than half, 87, were returned to their family, five were released on bail, eight were sent

to prison, 21 were married, 11 ran away, and 28 left for other reasons not mentioned in the report.[130] Thus two-thirds of the women
went back to the traditional way of solving problems: within the family or by marriage. This may not be an answer to their problems but
just a "suitable" way of dealing with women—the most "socially
acceptable" solution to their problems. The center could then be regarded as a kind of intermediary to reconcile families, and in a
sense fulfill one of its goals, namely, to return the woman to her
family, and ipso facto to society. However, in terms of rehabilitation,
very little can effectively be achieved under the existing structures
of the centers.

CONCLUSION

This chapter has dealt with the Libyan woman in the last decade.
It has attempted to show how far she has advanced from a very conservative background and what problems she faces in a rapidly developing society. It is perhaps the interrelationship of the two forces of
traditionalism and modernism in conflict that has created many of the
"problems" Libyan women have had to deal with at every stage of
their life. It is when roles are no longer clearly defined, positions
within a social framework no longer allotted on the basis of certain
ascribed (or achieved) criteria, that difficulties arise. And dialec-
tically, it is from those difficulties and from those conflicts that new
values, new relationships, and new patterns of living emerge that are
more appropriate to a changing environment.

It is with this in mind that we have tried in this chapter to view
women in Libya at each stage of life—childhood, marriage, divorce,
occupation, education, and even deviance—and to reveal the conflicting forces that are pushing them forward and simultaneously holding
them back, giving them opportunities and limiting their achievements,
revealing to them the undreamed of liberties of women in other societies only to make their own limited freedom harder for them to
bear, and displaying new ways of living for which they will have to
pay dearly to achieve. Nowhere has contemporary woman been asked
to change so quickly in so little time than in Libya, and nowhere are
the forces of society so strong in keeping her in a traditionally submissive position. Although in other countries of the Arab world
women are still very much locked into traditional structures, it is
only in Libya that the political and the social institutions are each
pulling women in opposite directions, each for its own ends—the
social institutions in order to keep the status quo, the government in
order to be able to use women as a political basis, both active and
vocal, to boost its legitimacy.[131]

NOTES

1. Christiane Souriau, "La Societe Feminine en Libye," Revue de l'Occident Musulman et de la Mediterranee 16 (1er et 2em trimestre 1969): 128-29.

2. International Bank for Reconstruction and Development, The Economic Development of Libya (Baltimore: Johns Hopkins Press, 1960), p. 252.

3. Socialist People's Libyan Arab Jamahiriya (SPLAJ), Secretariat of Planning, Al-Ihsa'at al-Hayawiya 1396 AH, 1976 AD (Tripoli, n.d. [1978?]), Table 1, p. 1.

4. SPLAJ, Secretariat of Planning, Al-Ihsa'at al-Hayawiya 1395 AH, 1975 AD (Tripoli, n.d.), Table 1, p. 1.

5. SPLAJ, Secretariat of Planning, Al-Ihsa'at al-Hayawiya 1394 AH, 1974 AD (Tripoli, n.d.), Table 1, p. 1.

6. International Labor Office (ILO), "Demographic Trends in Libya 1954-1978," Project of Planning and Evaluation of the Workforce in Libya, mimeographed (Tripoli, 1968), p. 7.

7. Ibid., p. 8.

8. Libyan Arab Republic (LAR), Secretariat of Planning, Al-Ihsa'at al-Hayawiya 1393 AH, 1973 AD (Tripoli, n.d.), Table 6, p. 10; Table 13, p. 23.

9. LAR, Al-Ihsa'at al-Hayawiya, 1975, Table 22, p. 42; Al-Ihsa'at al-Hayawiya, 1976, Table 22, p. 42.

10. World Health Organization (WHO), World Health Statistics, vol. I (Geneva, 1977), Table 7, p. 160.

11. Ibid., Table 7, p. 272.

12. Ibid., Table 7, p. 312.

13. Ibid., Table 7, p. 496.

14. Ibid., Table 7, p. 416.

15. Ibid., Table 7, p. 400.

16. Our calculations based on LAR, Al-Ihsa'at al-Hayawiya, 1976, Table 22, p. 42.

17. See Souriau, p. 135.

18. LAR, Al-Ihsa' at al-Hayawiya, 1976, Table 22, p. 42.

19. Ibid.

20. SPLAJ, Secretariat of Planning, Census and Statistics Department, Population Census Summary Data 1393 AH, 1973 AD (Tripoli, n.d.), Table 19, p. 19.

21. Ibid.

22. LAR, Ministry of Planning, Census and Statistics Department, Al-Ihsa'at al-Hayawiya 1392 AH, 1972 AD (Tripoli, n.d.), Table 6, p. 10; Al-Ihsa'at al-Hayawiya, 1973, Table 6, p. 10; and Al-Ihsa'at al-Hayawiya, 1974, Table 6, p. 10.

23. LAR, Al-Ihsa' at al-Hayawiya, 1972, Table 6, p. 10.

24. Ibid.

25. In rural areas the mahr includes agricultural and animals products, and often silver instead of gold. Among the nomads the mahr will also involve the gift of cattle and sheep, grain, and silver. 'Ali al-Fenaish, Al-Mujtama' al-Libi wa Mushkilatihi (Tripoli, 1967), pp. 47-48.

26. I am grateful to Mufida al-Bahi for her explanation of the various ways in which the mahr can be made to include the gifts or the furniture of the house or economic assets other than just a lump sum of money. What is included must be spelled out in the marriage contract.

27. In the Fezzan it is not unusual for a young man who wishes to marry to prepare a house and furnish it completely (and even to include a female wardrobe), and then to proceed to find a bride through the complex channels of relatives and intermediaries. Al-Fenaish, p. 48.

28. "Hatta la Nasil ila al-Tariq al-Masdud," al-Bayt 13 (October 5, 1977): 32.

29. For marriage customs see al-Fenaish, pp. 46-61.

30. Ibid., pp. 47-48.

31. Souriau, p. 131. She quotes a Libyan journalist writing in Libya al-Haditha 6 (August 20, 1968): 26.

32. Al-Fenaish, p. 48.

33. See Jamil Hilal, Dirasat fi al-Waqi' al-Libi (Tripoli: Maktabat al-Fikr, n.d. [1967?]).

34. Hilal, table on p. 85. Our averages were based on his figures for the three tribes of Masrata.

35. Ibid.

36. See al-Fenaish, pp. 46-51.

37. Population Census Summary Data, Table 28, p. 28.

38. Hilal, p. 95.

39. Ibid., pp. 95-96.

40. Al-Fajr al-Jadid (Tripoli), July 5, 1978, p. 4.

41. Article 1 of the Law No. 176 of the year 1392 AH, 1972 AD, Official Gazette 10 (December 23, 1972): 3076.

42. Ibid., Article 2, of the Law No. 176, p. 3077.

43. Ibid., Article 3, of the Law No. 176.

44. Al-Ihsa'at al-Hayawiya, 1972, Table 21; Tables 31 and 32 in Al-Ihsa'at al-Hayawiya, 1973, 1974, 1975, 1976.

45. Hilal, pp. 89-93.

46. See, for example, the monthly magazine Al-Mar'a published in Tripoli, 1976-present.

47. Chapter 2, al-Tatliq lil-idrar, an explanation of the Law No. 176, in a pamphlet (with no title) published by the LAR, Ministry of Justice, on laws No. 112 of 1971, No. 176 of 1972, and No. 18 of 1973.

48. Ibid., pp. 21-24. See also Ann Mayer, "Developments in the Law of Marriage and Divorce in Libya since the 1969 Revolution," Journal of African Law 22 (Spring 1978): 30-42.

49. See Articles 12-19 of the Law No. 176 in the Official Gazette 10 (December 23, 1972): 3079-81.

50. Mu'ammar al-Qadhdhafi, Al-Sijil al-Qawmi Bayanat, wa Khutab, wa Ahadith 1976-1977, vol. 8 (Tripoli, n.d.), p. 622.

51. al-Qadhdhafi, Thawrat al-Sha'b al-Libi (Tripoli, 1974), p. 403.

52. See al-Qadhdhafi's address to the Women's Union in Cairo on July 5, 1973, in Al-Sijil al-Qawmi, Bayanat, wa Khutab, wa Ahadith 1972-1973, vol. 4 (Tripoli, n.d.), p. 1236.

53. This legislation was passed by the General Popular Committee and the text published in Al-Bayt 13 (October 20, 1977): 6.

54. LAR, Ministry of Health, Al-Khadamat al-Sihhiya fi Saba' Sanawat 1389-1396 AH, 1969-1976 AD (Tripoli, n.d.), pp. 78-80.

55. Nisa' al-Jamahiriya, pamphlet (Tripoli, February 1978), p. 18.

56. Siba al-Fahoum, La Femme Lybienne en Dix Ans 1965-1975 (Beirut: The Lebanese Branch of the World Feminine League for Peace and Freedom, n.d.), p. 67.

57. Ibid., p. 68.

58. Quoted in ibid., p. 69.

59. Ibid., pp. 70-71.

60. LAR, Ministry of Planning and Scientific Research, Al-Majmu'a al-Ihsa'iya 1393 AH, 1973 AD (Tripoli: Government Press, 1975), Table 1, p. 54.

61. LAR, Al-Ihsa'at al-Hayawiya, 1973, Table 3, p. 6.

62. University of Benghazi, Research Center, Lamha 'an al-Wadi' al-Iqtisadi wal-Ijtima'i lil-Mar'a fi al-Jumhuriya al-'Arabiya al-Libiya (Benghazi, 1975), Table 9, p. 32.

63. Quoted in al-Fahoum, p. 52.

64. Ibid.

65. Ibid., Article 95, of the Law on Work No. 58, of 1970, p. 53. "This kind of work destroys her femininity, beauty and nature . . .," states al-Qadhdhafi in "Women's Rights," Jamahiriya Review (August 1980), p. 8.

66. Article No. 44 of Law No. 6 of 1958, amended on August 16, 1961, quoted in University of Benghazi, Lamha 'an al-Wadi' al-Iqtisadi wal-Ijtima'i lil Mar'a, p. 14.

67. Based on the Social Security Law No. 53 of 1957, amended by the Law No. 21 of 1962 and Law No. 72 of 1973. Quoted in LAR, General Women's Association, Al-Mar'a fi al-Tashri'at al-'Arabiya al-Libiya, pamphlet (n.p., n.d.).

68. Ibid.

69. Ibid.

70. Ibid., Article 23 of the Law on Work No. 58 of 1970.

71. Population Census Summary Data, p. 10.

72. Ibid., figure based on Table 3, p. 3 and Table 4, p. 4.

73. Ibid., Table 8, p. 8.

74. SPLAJ, Secretariat of Planning, Census and Statistics Department, Nata' ij al-Ta' dad al-'Am lil-Sukkan 1393 AH, 1973 AD, Al-Zawiya (Tripoli: Government Press, 1977), Table 60, p. 115.

75. SPLAJ, Secretariat of Planning, Census and Statistics Department, Nata'ij al-Ta' dad al-' Am lil-Sukkan 1393 AH, 1973 AD, Gharyan (Tripoli: Government Press, 1977), Table 60, p. 115.

76. SPLAJ, Secretariat of Planning, Census and Statistics Department, Nata' ij al-Ta 'dad al-' Am lil-Sukkan 1393 AH, 1973 AD, Al-Khalij (Tripoli: Government Press, 1977), Table 60, p. 112.

77. J. A. Allan, K. S. McLacklan et al., eds., Libya: Agriculture and Economic Development (London: Frank Cass, 1973), pp. 158-59.

78. Population Census Summary Data, Table 3, p. 3.

79. Ibid., Table 31, p. 31.

80. Our calculations are based on SPLAJ, Secretariat of Planning, Census and Statistics Department, Nata'ij al-Ta' dad al-'Am lil-Sukkan 1393 AH, 1973 AD, 10 vols.: Tripoli, Darna, Benghazi, Al-Zawiya, Al-Khalij, Sabha, Masrata, Gharyan, Khums, Al-Jabal al-Akhdar (Tripoli: Government Press, 1977). See Table 13 in each volume.

81. Ibid.

82. Ibid.

83. Ibid., Table 84 in all ten volumes.

84. ILO, "Demographic Trends in Libya 1954-1978," p. 8.

85. Ibid., p. 7.

86. The figure 80,546 is 18.6 percent of the total rural female population of 432,983 and 5,473 is 18.6 percent of 30,408.

87. Population Census Summary Data, Table 22, p. 22.

88. Ibid., the total Libyan economically active population being 415,560.

89. Al-Fahoum, pp. 71-72.

90. SPLAJ, Council for Reclamation of Land, Executive Committee for Sahl al-Jafara, Al-Mar'a wal-Thawra al-Zira' iya fi al-Rif, pamphlet (Tripoli: Matba' at al-Rif, 1977), p. 15.

91. From a conversation with Mustafa O. Attir, chairman of the Sociology Department, Al-Fateh University, April 1978.

92. University of Benghazi, Lamha 'an al-Wadi' al-Iqtisadi wal-Ijtima'i lil-Mar'a, p. 15.

93. LAR, Ministry of Culture and Education, Taqrir 'an Qita al-Ta' lim wal-Tarbiya min 68/69 ila 1975, pamphlet (n.p., n.d.), table on p. 12.

94. LAR, Ministry of Culture and Education, Department of Planning and Development, Ihsa' at al-Ta' lim fi al-Jumhuriya al-'Arabiya al-Libiya 'an al-'Am al-Dirasi 1394-1395 AH, 1974-1975 AD (Tripoli: Government Press, n.d.), tables on pp. 39, 67, 95, on which our calculations are based.

95. Ibid.

96. Population Census Summary Data, Table 3, p. 3.

97. We are indebted to Mufida al-Bahi for her explanation.

98. Our calculations based on Ihsa' at al-Ta' lim, 1974-1975, table on p. 18.

99. See the report on those centers in SPLAJ, Al-Mar' a wal-Thawra al-Zira' iya.

100. Al-Bayt 14 (February 5, 1978): 6-7.

101. SPLAJ, Al-Mar' a wal-Thawra al-Zira' iya, p. 30.

102. Ibid., p. 32.

103. Ibid., p. 27.

104. Ibid., pp. 34-35.

105. See Al-Fallah 17 (1977): 16-17 for a specimen of the material taught in those centers, and the home economics centers.

106. Eight centers are discussed in SPLAJ, Al-Mar' a fi al-Thawra al-Zira' iya, pp. 50-70.

107. LAR, Council for Rural Development, Ma' a Masira al-Tanmiya al-Zira' iya al-Mutakamila (Tripoli, 1976), p. 22.

108. This number may be higher as there were 45 unmarried girls who enrolled in the Al-Amal Center of Qarbulli in 1976 and who were not included in the figures above. LAR, Council for Rural Development, Ma' Munjazat Mashru' Wadi al-Raml Al-Qarbulli (Tripoli, n.d. [1976?]), p. 24.

109. See SPLAJ, Secretariat of Agriculture, Munjazat al-Thawra al-Zira' iya fi Majal al-Zira' a, vol. 4 (Tripoli, n.d. [1978?]), pp. 166-67.

110. Al-Fallah 4 (1975): 30.

111. Nisa' al-Jamahiriya 1 (February 1978): 27.

112. Al-Fallah 4 (1975): 30.

113. Al-Fallah 1 (1978): 58-59.

114. SPLAJ, Secretariat of the Interior, General Directorate for Security Affairs, Center for Research in Criminology, Taqrir 'an Halat al-Jarima 1396 AH, 1976 AD (Tripoli, n.d. [1978?]), Table 9, p. 19.

115. Ibid.

116. Ibid.

117. Ibid.

118. The study that we were not able to obtain was published by the Society of the New Woman in Benghazi in 1974, in Arabic, and is entitled Problems of Women Prisoners and Some Solutions.

119. Al-Fahoum, p. 89.

120. Ibid.

121. LAR, Ministry for Social Affairs and Social Security, Dalil al-Ihsa' at al-Ijtima' iya 1394 AH, 1974 AD, vol. 1 (Tripoli, n.d.), p. 119.

122. Ibid.

123. See SPLAJ, Secretariat for Social Affairs and Social Security, Dalil al-Ihsa' at al-Ijtima' iya 1395 AH, 1975 AD, vol. 2 (Tripoli, n.d.), Table 94, p. 132.

124. LAR, Ministry for Social Affairs and Social Security, Munjazat Wizarat al-Shu' un al-Ijtima' iya wal-Daman al-Ijtima' i, 1396 AH, 1976 AD (Tripoli, n.d. [1976?]), p. 24.

125. SPLAJ, The Secretariat for Social Affairs and Social Security, Al-Kitab al-Sanawi li-Munjazat 1397 AH, 1977 AD (Tripoli, n.d. [1978]), p. 21.

126. Dalil al-Ihsa' at al-Ijtima' iya, 1975, Table 96, p. 134.

127. Ibid., Table 104, p. 137.

128. Ibid., Table 105, p. 137.

129. Ibid., Table 96, p. 134.

130. Ibid., Table 100, p. 135.

131. See the statement on the political role of women in "Ikhtitam A' mal al-Multaqa al-Awal li-Lijan al-Thawriya al-Nisa' iya bi-Hay al-Andalus," Al-Zahf al-Akhdar, August 11, 1980, p. 14.

Chapter 4

ISLAM IN REVOLUTIONARY LIBYA

This chapter discusses the extent to which Islam has played a role in the revolutionary ideology of Libya since 1969, placing it in historical perspective especially with respect to the Sanusiya movement. Mu'ammar al-Qadhdhafi's revolutionary conception of Islam will be examined and categorized in the light of the fundamentalism-reformism dichotomy.[1]

Islam in revolutionary Libya cannot be understood without examining its historical roots, which go back to the Sanusiya movement, and viewing it within the framework of the region as a whole. We maintain that the Sunni Muslim variant of Islamic fundamentalism in the Arab world arose in two distinct sociopolitical environments. The first was that of the basically tribal settled and semisettled societies threatened by changes taking place both in the socioeconomic and the political spheres. In that type of sociopolitical environment there emerged three kinds of tribal-based Muslim fundamentalist movements that were strengthened by the existence of a dominant alien power. The puritan and unitarian Wahhabi movement, which subscribed to the Hanbalite school of jurisprudence and was anti-Sufist and against the religious establishment, represented by the Ottoman Empire, was one such movement that emerged in the heartland of the Arabian peninsula in Najd. The second kind of tribal-based fundamentalism, which was strongly associated with a Sufi order or tariqa and acquired a clearer and more distinct form when it encountered an alien colonizer, was the Sanusiya movement in Libya. The Sudanese Mahdiya movement represents a third kind of tribal-based Muslim fundamentalism that existed on the frontiers of Islam[2] and was strengthened by its struggle against non-Muslim colonizers as well as by its efforts to spread the call of Islam beyond its borders.

The second sociopolitical environment that gave rise to Muslim fundamentalism in the Arab world emerged among some members of the disenchanted and to some extent uprooted petite bourgeoisie of urban centers and particularly of small towns. This was the social origin of the society of the Muslim Brothers in Egypt, and later in Palestine, Sudan, and Syria.

It is within that geopolitical and religious context that Libya's particular brand of Islamic fundamentalism should be viewed. Libya witnessed, from the mid-nineteenth century and up to the early 1930s when Italy's occupation of Libya was completed, a fundamentalist movement of its own: the Sanusiya movement. Although this movement was not entirely confined to Libya, it was organized and led from the eastern provinces of Libya in Jaghbub and in Kufra at a later stage, and its largest following and most numerous zawiyas were in Libya as well. Thus Islam in Libya was inexorably linked to the Sanusiya movement, which was not simply a fundamentalist movement or a salafiya movement, but contained both fundamentalist and reformist elements within it. These two elements are discernible both in the ideology and the practice of the Sanusiya. An example of the fundamentalist element in the Sanusi ideology can be traced to the tremendous influence of Ibn Taymiya (the Muslim jurist and political thinker) on the movement (an influence which was similar to that on the Wahhabi movement). Thus according to the Grand Sanusi Saiyyid Muhammad 'Ali al-Sanusi the Qur'an and the Sunna constituted the basis of Islam while qiyas and ijma' were rejected. On the other hand, unlike the Wahhabis, the Sanusis did not follow the Hanbalite school of jurisprudence, but simply played down the role of the various schools of jurisprudence, which in effect meant playing down the role of the Malikite school, which was the dominant school in Libya at the time.

The Sanusiya movement passed through three historical stages. The first stage was that of the rise and expansion of the movement during the leadership of the Grand Sanusi, the founder of the movement, who died in 1859, and that of his son Sayyid al-Mahdi, who died in 1902. During that period, which began with the first Sanusi zawiya in Libya established in al-Bayda' in Cyrenaica in 1843, the founder of the movement had a vision that included the whole Muslim world. The movement originated in the realization by the Grand Sanusi that the Ottoman Empire had become weak and was no longer able to defend the Muslims from European encroachments (as in the case of the French invasion in 1830 of Algeria, the Grand Sanusi's home country). Moreover, he felt that the modernizing policies of Muhammad 'Ali that he had witnessed in Egypt were undermining the position of the 'ulama', a fact that further convinced him of the need for reform (islah) of the Muslim world.[3] During this first stage,

both the Grand Sanusi and his son Sayyid al-Mahdi aimed at the unification of Muslim orders as a preparatory stage for the unification of
all Muslims. The objectives at this stage were missionary, directed
toward Muslims, who were only nominally so, and appealing to the
pastoral-tribal population of Cyrenaica, and its strict moral code
and austerity. This missionary zeal was also directed toward non-
Muslim pagans in the Sudan and Central Africa, and in fact gained
many converts to Islam among them. The vision of the Sanusi leadership was then pan-Islamic, and the movement became important
enough to draw the attention of the Ottoman authorities, especially
during the reign of 'Abd al-Hamid II. This in turn gave rise to the
need for the Sanusis to isolate themselves in order to keep their
freedom of action and not be used by the Ottomans or others, and
thus deviate from their own purposes. The moving of their headquarters in 1895 from Jaghbub to the more isolated Kufra oasis was
significant and symbolic of the change taking place in the goals of the
Sanusiya. The members became gradually more parochial in their
activities and aims, appealing now primarily to some tribes in certain regions of Cyrenaica and southeastern Libya. Here we come to
one of the basic features of this kind of Muslim fundamentalism,
namely, its tribal base. In the Sanusiya movement the Khaldunian
symbiosis of the religious 'asabiya or esprit de corps with the tribal
'asabiya became complete. It was only at times of favorable political
and military conditions that the movement encompassed some rural
and urban areas as well. The Sanusiya movement differed from the
Wahhabiya movement because it did not seek to realize its goals
through military actions. The 'alim-sufi (as the Grand Sanusi and
his successors were called) kept tight control over the Sanusi movement, while the tribal leadership of Ibn Sa'ud prevailed in the case
of the Wahhabi movement. The Sanusiya sought to achieve its objectives through peaceful peans, and only took arms to defend itself and
its territory when faced with French expansionism in the south from
1901 onward and Italian imperialism in the north with their invasion
of Libya in September 1911.

The beginning of the second historical stage of the Sanusiya
movement may be said to have coincided with the emergence of the
leadership of Ahmad al-Sharif in 1902, continued through that of
al-Sayyid Idris after World War I, and lasted until the independence
of Libya in December 1951. During this second stage, the Sanusiya
movement, which by then had a tremendous following among the tribes
of Cyrenaica and some influence among the tribes of Sirtica, Tripolitania, and Fazzan, was transformed from a religious movement into
a primarily political and national movement. It allied itself, under
Sayyid Idris, to a European power, Great Britain, against another one,
Italy, and eventually its objectives ceased to be universal and

acquired a parochial and territorial dimension. From 1917 onward it led the resistance movement against the Italians, especially during the Italo-Sanusi war of 1923-32. Although by 1932 Libya had been completely occupied and subdued, the Sanusi zawiyas had been closed, and the property of the movement confiscated, the Sanusi leadership continued to be regarded as the major political leadership of Libya in exile.[4] In fact Sayyid Idris, the Sanusi leader, had become the uncontested leader of Cyrenaica, although only reluctantly accepted by the notables and leaders of Tripolitania. This uneven support that Sayyid Idris had in the two major regions of Libya was of tremendous importance in enhancing further the political character of the Sanusiya at the expense of its religious character. More Tripolitanians, especially among the urban and rural population, were willing to accept Sayyid Idris as the leader of the resistance against the Italian occupation and therefore as a national leader, rather than as the head of a religious order or movement. The Italians had thus rendered Sayyid Idris a service, for, as E. E. Evans-Pritchard stated, "As events turned out, the Italians, by destroying the Sanusiya organization, cut out the intervening structure of the lodges and Shaiks and made more evident the political status of the Head of the Order."[5] Thus Sayyid Idris inherited the Sanusi 'asabiya, which was religious founded on a tribal base, but during the period of the struggle against the Italians he added a "national" dimension to his leadership, which had by then become basically mundane and secular in nature. Trying to appeal beyond his stronghold of Cyrenaica, Sayyid Idris sought political support from Tripolitania and Fazzan, and emerged as a national political leader who was to become the future constitutional monarch.

The third historical stage of the Sanusiya movement, which may be said to have begun in 1951 when Libya obtained its independence, was definitely characterized by the decline of the movement during the whole period of the monarchy between 1951 and 1969. During that period the Sanusiya movement ceased to be the focus of religious affairs and activities in Libya. It had historically created an 'asabiya that had united, in a way, the Sanusi Ikhwan around King Sayyid Idris, some of whom remained his closest associates during the whole period of the monarchy. Otherwise, the Sanusiya, as a politico-religious movement became a relic of the past. As early as October 1949, when the Constitution of Cyrenaica was promulgated, it stipulated that Islam was the religion of Cyrenaica and Arabic its official language, but no mention was made of the Sanusiya movement or its zawiyas, a fact pointing to the gradual trend toward greater secularism. In June 1954 the shari'a (canon law of Islam) courts were abolished as they had been in some other Arab countries, but due to popular pressure they were reinstated in October 1958. Majid Khadduri argues that the adopted judicial system was too advanced for Libya, and resentment in the rural and tribal areas in particular prompted the Libyan government to separate again the religious shari'a courts from the civil courts. [6]

During the first decade of independence there was not much emphasis placed on religious education, especially when compared to the 1960s. In November 1952, the king established in al-Bayda' the religious Institute of al-Sayyid Muhammad bin 'Ali al-Sanusi, named after the founder of the Sanusiya movement. At first the institute was under the supervision of the Ministry of Education in Cyrenaica, and only in 1958 did it acquire an autonomous character. Branches of it were established in other parts of Libya and incorporated into the already established religious institutions, such as that of Ahmad Pasha Karamanli in Tripoli and the Institute of Sidi 'Abd al-Salam al-Asmar in Zlitin.

The decade of the 1960s witnessed a greater shift toward religious education, especially during the period from 1961 to 1969. Other than the fact that the Libyan government had more funds to spend on education after the discovery of oil, there were two basic reasons for this revival in religious education. The first was the fear that the oil money and the gradual modernization that accompanied the economic development of the country was undermining the attachment of Libyans to traditional Muslim values in the society and would eventually lead to moral laxity. By 1961, the Higher Council of the Institute at al-Bayda' decided to open religious institutes in Gharyan, Zawiya, and Darna. In October 1962, the Institute at al-Bayda' was upgraded and changed into a Muslim university, incorporating various religious institutions in Tripoli, Zlitin, Zawiya, Sabha, and Darna as part of it. The enrollment in the religious educational institutions rose by leaps and bounds. By the mid-1960s enrollment in the Koranic schools rose from 3,735 students in 1960-61 to 6,082 in 1965-66, and in the Koranic recitation institutes from 35 to 62 during the same period. Elementary and secondary religious education enrollment also rose from 712 to 1,127, and at the higher institutes for religious education enrollment had increased from 35 students to 287 students also in the first half of the decade of the 1960s. [7]

Another basic reason for this greater emphasis on religious education in the 1960s and the attempt to reactivate and revive the Sanusi zawiyas[8] was the fear that the ideas of secular Arab nationalists of the Ba'th Party, the Arab Nationalist Movement, and of course those of Jamal 'Abd-al-Nasir would spread among the youth, especially the educated. Thus the emphasis on Islam and Islamic themes was seen by Arab conservative rulers as the best method to use to counterpoise the rising tide of secular Arab nationalism during that period.

In fact the challenge to the monarchic regime did not come directly from the secular Arab nationalists, whether of the Arab Socialist Ba'th Party or the Arab Nationalist Movement (ANM), although they laid the groundwork for it, but from a closely knit group of junior army officers led by al-Qadhdhafi, [9] who utilized the 'asabiya developed in the military college to successfully overthrow the regime. These junior army officers were influenced by the Arab nationalist thought of the Arab East through the broadcasts of the Voice of the Arabs from Cairo, and also through the literature of the Ba'th[10] and the ANM. However, they retained the strong Islamic identity of North African societies developed in their encounters with European colonization. Thus al-Qadhdhafi's conception of Islam is rooted in this amalgamation of the traditional Islamic identity and beliefs inculcated in his formative years, and the secular Arab nationalist identity that he imbibed from his readings of Arab nationalist ideologues. In this way, al-Qadhdhafi is at once a product and a reflection of the tension between these two world views.

The environment in which al-Qadhdhafi spent his formative years was characterized by the austerity and puritanism that is typical of a seminomadic milieu whether in Sirtica or in Fezzan. Most of his colleagues who formed the backbone of the Free Officers' Movement shared these values with him.[11] They took pride in the fact that they neither drank nor gambled. A strict moral code was adopted by them, and it was not surprising that when they came to power they issued a decree forbidding the consumption and the sale of alcoholic beverages and closed down all nightclubs that had existed primarily in Tripolitania. Both the seminomadic and the petit bourgeois backgrounds of the members of the Free Officers' Movement were congenial with the development of Muslim fundamentalism. However, their concern with symbols made them appear more fundamentalist than they really were, e.g., the issuing of a decree stating that the dates of the Hijra calendar[12] were to precede those of the Gregorian calendar on all official documents and that the signboards of all industrial and commercial institutions were to be written in Arabic only.

Due in part to the fact that al-Qadhdhafi hailed from Sirtica (at the periphery of the Sanusiya's radius of influence) and in part to the decline of the Sanusiya as a religious movement in the post World War II period, the ease with which he was able to transcend some of the Sanusi tenets can be more easily understood. Nevertheless, there remain some important continuities between the Sanusi doctrines and Islam in revolutionary Libya today.[13] A comparison between Islam in Libya in the 1970s and the Sanusiya legacy should first deal with their respective attitude toward what each considered the basis of Islam.

According to Sanusi doctrine, the Qur'an and the Sunna are the foundations of Islam, while the shari'a need not necessarily follow the Malikite school of jurisprudence. When al-Qadhdhafi came to power he wanted all legislation to be examined in the light of shari'a and consequently asked the Egyptian jurist 'Ali 'Ali Mansur in October 1969 to submit a study on Islamic shari'a and the way it could replace positive law in Libya. This document was completed a few months later in January 1970.[14] Mansur proposed gradualism in the application of Islamic shari'a, and advised retaining and not abolishing that body of positive law while concommitantly studying it to determine which legislations were contrary to Islamic shari'a, in order to promulgate new laws that would replace those deviating from shari'a.[15] Following the advice of the jurist Mansur, the Revolutionary Council issued a decree on October 28, 1978, stipulating that when new laws and legislation were promulgated, their conformity with the basic principles of shari'a had to be taken into consideration.[16] Committees were also instituted to review the existing laws and to examine whether those were in harmony with shari'a.[17] In reviewing the existing body of positive law, the explanatory memorandum that accompanied this decree made a distinction between two categories: doctrines (al-'aqa'id) and rites ('ibadat) on the one hand, and transactions (mu'amalat) and other matters of a more mundane nature on the other. The first category, it maintained, was not affected by time or place and therefore could not be interpreted, while the second changed with time and place, and varied with different environments and different customs, and consequently the mu'amalat in shari'a were to be seen as general principles of a flexible nature in the case of which the human mind could freely exercise its ability to choose and interpret.[18] We believe that in this dichotomy between doctrine and rites on the one hand and transactions on the other lies the germ of a functional secularism that developed more fully by the end of the 1970s.

In practice the review of positive law in Libya by the various committees meant that the changes made pertained only to flagrant contradictions to shari'a, such as laws concerning alcoholic drinks, adultery, the amendments in the penal code concerning punishment for theft, and so forth. Mansur admitted that most of the positive laws in practice in Libya were taken from the Egyptian civil code and were not in opposition to the basic principles of shari'a. After all, the civil code adopted by the Native Courts of Egypt since the late nineteenth century had been reviewed and basically approved by Azharite 'ulama' who represented the four schools of Sunni jurisprudence.[19] Consequently, the work of the Higher Committee, which was presided over by Mansur himself, and that of the three-branched committee that dealt with the personal status laws, the commercial civil code, and the penal code was limited to determining which laws or legislation were in opposition with the "absolute stipulations of Islamic shari'a" (al-ahkam al-qat'iya lil-shari'a), as in the case of commercial laws that dealt with usury (riba) between "natural persons" (al-ashkhas al-tabi'iyun) or usury on credit (bil-nasi'a).[20]

The studies done by the various committees for the review of positive law in Libya followed the basic principles of Islamic jurisprudence derived from the four schools of Sunni jurisprudence—the Hanafi, Maliki, Shafi'i, and Hanbali schools—as well as the two schools of Shi'ism—the Imami school and the Zaydi school—and finally also included the Ibadi and the Dhahiri schools. This open attitude with regard to all schools of jurisprudence and the refusal to be bound exclusively to the Maliki school of jurisprudence (the traditionally dominant one in Libya) was not unlike the attitude of the Sanusiya.

The Qur'an and the Sunna were regarded as the basis of Islam by the Sanusi and by al-Qadhdhafi as well until early 1978, when he began to play down the importance of the sunna* and in particular of the hadith.[†] As in the case of the Sanusi tradition, the door of ijtihad or interpretation remained open for al-Qadhdhafi and he stressed, as early as December 1970, the need to interpret Islam and interpret the Qur'an in a new manner. He maintained that although it was generally believed to be sinful to interpret the Qur'an, in fact "it is sinful not to interpret the Qur'an . . . and there should be an interpretation of every single verse of the Qur'an."[21] He contended that when this was done it could be shown that Islam was progressive and revolutionary. To him Islam is at once a mission of continuity (al-istimrar) that began with Prophet Muhammad and one of "permanent revolution" that has within it all the characteristics of a "modern ideology."[22] In other words, Islam to al-Qadhdhafi combines the isala (authenticity) rooted in tradition with the openness to new interpretations and its adaptation to the problems of the modern world.

One of the major problems that face scholars in categorizing religious movements and individual thinkers with respect to the fundamentalist-reformist dichotomy is the attitude of a particular movement or individual toward the role of the intermediaries between man and God. Emphasis on the transcendence of God has been generally associated with fundamentalism.[23] The Sanusiya movement could be

---

*The sunna are the deeds, utterances, and silent approval of the Prophet.

†The hadith is the record of the actions and the sayings of the Prophet.

regarded in this respect as part and parcel of the fundamentalist tradition. It is true that the Sanusiya movement emphasized the dual role
of the 'alim and the sufi, and the latter, in particular, did not lend
itself to a fundamentalist stand. Nevertheless, the fact that the
Sanusiya as a sufi order believed in establishing contacts with the
Muhammad and his immediate companions rather than with God re-
affirmed the element of transcendence with respect to the relationship
between man and God. Al-Qadhdhafi, on the other hand, rejected the
role of the sufi[24] and abolished the existing Sanusi zawiyas. Moreover,
he belittled the role of the 'alim and emphasized the direct relationship between man and God without any mediation.

During the period from early 1976 until the middle of 1978
al-Qadhdhafi's ideas on the foundation of Islam, Islamic jurisprudence
(fiqh), and the rule of both jurists (fuqaha') and men of religion
('ulama') shifted in the direction of the transcendence of God and the
virtual elimination of intermediaries between man and God. Al-
Qadhdhafi maintained by early 1976 that the Qur'an ought to be the
direct source of legislation because all other sources were liable to
error as their origin was human and not divine. Moreover, he claimed,
the Qur'an itself might have been distorted by the jurists' interpretation. Being human, the jurists could be subject to human vagaries
and influences unrelated to religious thought. Consequently, he concluded, the practices and beliefs of Muslims today were not in complete harmony with the basic precepts of Islam due in part to the
distorting influence of the jurists' interpretations, which were strict
at times and lenient at others, depending on their individual state of
being rather than on the subject matter of their interpretation.[25] The
virtual dismissal of the role of the intermediary is clearly revealed
in a statement by al-Qadhdhafi made in a speech delivered on the
anniversary of the Prophet, February 19, 1978: "The Qur'an is in
the Arabic language and we can therefore comprehend it ourselves
without the need for an imam to interpret it for us."[26] In the same
speech, al-Qadhdhafi affirmed that the Qur'an was the essence of
Islam, and that the Prophet was only a human being, the messenger
of God. Therefore the hadith was not to be regarded as binding on
Muslims as the Prophet himself had never asked Muslims to follow
the hadith. Moreover, al-Qadhdhafi pointed out that if the hadith was
regarded to be as sacred as the Qur'an by Muslims, then they would
be committing the sin of shirk.[27] It was therefore possible to discuss
the hadith and accept or reject any part of it because it did not have
a divine origin, especially those parts of it that were of doubtful
authenticity and had been attributed to the Prophet by individuals with
ulterior motives. Al-Qadhdhafi also criticized the habit of some Muslims to quote from the hadith, to visit the shrines of saints, and to
fear Muhammad at times even more than they feared God, all actions

that distorted religion and the very essence of Islam. In another speech on July 3, 1978, he depicted Islamic jurisprudence as not unlike positive law (al-qanun al-wad'i). He also went beyond his earlier idea and asserted that the Qur'an was the only source of shari'a.

This greater transcendence in the relationship between man and God is not a fundamentalist stand, [28] but according to al-Qadhdhafi, it is a necessary precondition for reformative (islahiya) and renovative (tajdidiya) revolutions in Islam, a kind of Protestantism that bypasses all intermediaries between man and God. [29] This view is in sharp contrast with that of the Sanusi tradition of establishing mystical contacts with the Prophet and his immediate companions. The only contact with the Prophet that is retained in al-Qadhdhafi's view of Islam is the intellectual one via the medium of discussion and debate, with respect to the Sunna and in particular to the hadith.

The implications of these views point clearly to a de facto functional secularism that would curb the role of the 'ulama' and the fuqaha'. As early as May 1975, al-Qadhdhafi maintained that mundane matters ought to be separated from otherworldly matters in the Friday prayer in mosques. People, he argued, were busy the whole week with mundane matters and needed to listen to something else in the Friday sermon. Quoting from the Qur'an, al-Wadhdhafi said, "O believers, when proclamation is made for prayer on the Day of Congregation, hasten to God's remembrance, "[30] adding that instead people went to the mosques on Fridays to hear the imam speak about housing problems, bank loans, the building of roads, and so forth. Such matters he maintained were better discussed in political meetings or the mass media. On May 2, 1975, al-Qadhdhafi addressed himself to all the imams of the mosques in the country, stating that "Sermons on Fridays must deal with those matters which man has come to the mosque to seek, which are prayer and God's remembrance, only."[31]

The major criticism leveled by al-Qadhdhafi against men of religion concerned their rigidity in the interpretation of religion (al-tazammut). That, he argued, could lead people to become antireligious, as had been the case in Christianity when the rigidity in interpretation and the corruption of the Catholic church had given rise to Protestantism and eventually to atheistic ideologies like communism. In addition, Al-Qadhdhafi reminded the Libyan 'ulama' and the fuqaha' that Atatürk's anticlericalism had been due to the rigidity of the Muslim 'ulama' in his time.

His admiration for Atatürk was based first on the fact that Atatürk was an army man and as an army officer he had fought the Italians in Libya, and second, and perhaps even more significantly, al-Qadhdhafi's relationship to the 'ulama' and fuqaha' was mutatis mutandis, similar to that of Atatürk's when he tried to implement his reforms. The men of religion in Libya felt threatened by al-Qadhdhafi's radicalism, while he strongly attacked them, describing them as a reactionary group who distorted Islam and made it rigid. This attack culminated in the purging in May-June 1978 of the imams who were critical of him and his policies from mosques in Tripoli, Benghazi, Tajura, Zuwara, and Khums.

Al-Qadhdhafi's de facto functional secularism and his anti-clericalism affected his ideological stand as well with respect to various political parties and groups in the Arab world. By September 1975 he was willing to cooperate with Arab Communists and other Arab leftist movements because, as he expressed his position, "economics is unrelated to believing in God."[32]

By the summer of 1980 al-Qadhdhafi was maintaining that his Green Book, with its three chapters in which he expounded his political, economic, and social views, was unrelated to Islam in the sense that his Third Theory, the alternative to capitalism and communism, was not Islamic in character. According to him, "The Green Book does not state that Islam should be the religion, or the Qur'an the shari'a" of any particular society.[33] The Third Theory, he claims, was simply the outcome of man's effort to resolve his problems, irrespective of the specific historical epoch or the particular society in which he lived. This is in direct contrast to his earlier assertions that his Third Theory was basically rooted in Islam.[34] Is this an inconsistency or is it a change that took place in al-Qadhdhafi's attitude toward Islam as a universal religion? In 1973 al-Qadhdhafi maintained that "Islam is neither an Arab nor an Eastern religion, but an international and universal mission."[35] On the other hand, he also regarded Islam as national in character in the sense that the Arab lands had been the land of the prophets, the Arabic language the language of the Qur'an, and the Arabs had been chosen to carry this message. It is al-Qadhdhafi's attempt to reconcile the nationalist and the universal conceptions of Islam without abandoning either that have led him to oscillate from one conception to the other, depending on the situation encountered.

His oscillations could be clearly seen in his attitude toward non-Muslim minorities in the Arab world. For al-Qadhdhafi, brought up in a society that did not encompass religious divisions among its indigenous population, it was difficult for him to conceive of an Arab society that had divisions of a sectarian or religious nature. He admitted that the only Christians he had ever seen or met in the desert where he had been brought up were the Christian colonizers, whether Italian or British.[36] Consequently, coming from such a background it was understandable that his conception of Arab nationalism or Arabism was simply tied to his Islamic identity. He was criticized for that by Arabs from the Eastern part of the Arab world who saw his beliefs as a divisive influence that could alienate non-Sunni Muslims as well as Christian Arabs.

As a reaction to this criticism al-Qadhdhafi put forward his all-inclusive view of Islam. To him Islam includes the "people of the Book," all those who believe in God and His prophets are Muslims, and consequently, Christians and Jews were Muslims even before the coming of Prophet Muhammad.[37] He believes that the adoption of an all-inclusive view of Islam would make it possible to transcend divisions based on religious and sectarian grounds. This conception of Islam, however, is not new. It was expressed in the writings of such intellectuals of the Arab East as Zaki al-Arsuzi, the Syrian ideologue of the Ba'th, and Antun Sa'adah, the founder of the ideology of Syrian nationalism, in his al-Islam fi Risalatayhi al-Muhammadiya wal-Masihiya.

Al-Qadhdhafi, however, did express on occasion intolerance toward the Christian minorities in the Arab world. At times, for instance, he has depicted the conflict in Lebanon as basically one between Christians and Muslims[38] and has stated that if it were not for the existence there of the Christian Arabs, there would have been no conflict.[39] In an interview published in the Lebanese daily al-Safir, al-Qadhdhafi reverted back to the nationalist dimension of Islam, illustrating Albert Hourani's insightful statement about the Turkish and Arab nations: ". . . by what might seem almost a paradox, while the religious link between one nation and another vanished, the relationship within each national community, between religion and nation still persisted."[40] Al-Qadhdhafi maintained that Christian Arabs would not be true Arabs until they became Muslims because "Prophet Muhammad had been sent to the Arabs with an Arab tongue and an Arab Qur'an."[41] The Christian Arab—who was, according to al-Qadhdhafi, closer to the Vatican than he was to Mecca—was plagued by a duality (izdiwajiya) in identity that prevented him from becoming a full member of the Arab nation as his religion was not the religion of that nation. "Nationalism and religion," he maintained, "are the two facets of the same coin."[42] Statements of the sort, however, do not make al-Qadhdhafi a pan-Islamist. On the contrary, at times he appeared quite the opposite, accusing the non-Arab Muslims of distorting the Qur'an and emphasizing that their role historically had been that of volunteers, or auxiliaries (mutatawi'un) to the cause of Islam.[43]

It is interesting to note another paradox in al-Qadhdhafi's thoughts on religion: as he became more anticlerical and secular, preaching a "protestantism" of Islam and separating his political and social ideology from that of Islam, he compensated for this by a stronger attachment to Islam as an integral and inseparable part of his communal identity.

In conclusion, al-Qadhdhafi's conception of Islam could be said to be rooted in the Sanusi tradition but has gone beyond it and transcended it gradually over the past decade. His rejection of tazammut or the rigidity in interpretation of religion shows his openness to outside influences, and his insistence on the importance of the progressive role of Islam makes him a Muslim reformist, while the fact that he no longer tied his social and political ideology to Islam is also an illustration of his functional secularism. As a protagonist of his regime stated, "Islam is not the ideology of the Mass Republic of Libya, what we are saying is that our understanding of Islam and of the Qur'an are [forever] changing and renewing themselves."[44]

Al-Qadhdhafi's emphasis that the Qur'an is the only source of shari'a and that those parts of the hadith that do not tally with the Qur'an ought to be rejected is also reformist in implication: a return to the source, a protestant reformism of Islam.[45] Similarly, his insistence on the transcendence of God and the purely human role of the Prophet as an intermediary between God and man could be compared to the views held by the Hanbalite and other fundamentalist schools of thought. However, both his reformism and his fundamentalism were brought about, in part at least, by purely practical considerations: his desire to limit the role of the 'ulama' and to encourage a gradual de facto secularism at the expense of their power.

Al-Qadhdhafi oscillates between Islam as a universal religion and Islam as the national religion of the Arabs, with a greater emphasis on the latter in recent times. This shows the importance given by al-Qadhdhafi to cultural unity within the Arab nation (and its adverse implications for religious minorities) on the one hand, and the recognition of cultural diversity beyond the Arab community in the Muslim world on the other, a stand that is not usually in harmony with that of Muslim fundamentalists.

Finally, one can conclude that the only purely fundamentalist element in the practice of Islam for al-Qadhdhafi has been his strict adherence to shari'a with respect to alcoholic drinks, gambling, prostitution, and so forth. Although these are necessary ingredients of fundamentalism, they are also, in the case of al-Qadhdhafi, an outcome of the austere and puritan spirit that the desert and its habitat frequently inspires. For al-Qadhdhafi in particular, the desert has been the source of creativity and continuity, and therefore looms large in both his conception of Islam and his general social and political ideology, with which we shall deal in Chapter 5.

NOTES

1. See, for example, John Voll, "The Sudanese Mahdi: Frontier Fundamentalist," International Journal of Middle East Studies 10 (May 1979): 145-66.

2. See L. Carl Brown, "The Sudanese Mahdiya," in Protest and Power in Black Africa, eds. Robert I. Rotberg and Ali A. Mazrui (New York: Oxford University Press, 1970), pp. 145-68, especially, pp. 160-61, 167-68.

3. Muhammad Fu'ad Shukri, Al-Sanusiya Din wa Dawla (Cairo: Dar al-Fikr al-'Arabi, 1948), pp. 16-18.

4. E. E. Evans-Pritchard, The Sanusi of Cyrenaica (Oxford: Clarendon Press, 1949), pp. 193-94.

5. Ibid., p. 228.

6. Majid Khadduri, Modern Libya a Study in Political Development (Baltimore: Johns Hopkins Press, 1963), pp. 199-200.

7. Kingdom of Libya, Al-Ta'lim al-Dini fi Libya (Tripoli: Wizarat al-I'lam, 1966), p. 24. For 1968-69, see chap. 2, p. 74.

8. Khadduri, p. 332.

9. Al-Qadhdhafi entered military college in October 1963 and graduated in August 1965.

10. Al-Qadhdhafi admitted the influence of Michel 'Aflaq's book Ma'rakat al-Masir al-Wahid on his ideas. Min Ahadith al-'Aqid Mu'ammar al-Qadhdhafi fi al-Sahafa al-'Arabiya wal-'Alamiya from August 2 1973 to April 29, 1974 (Tripoli: Al-Thawra al-'Arabiya Press, n.d.), p. 29.

11. For the social background of the 12 members of the Revolutionary Command Council of the Free Officers Movement see Ruth First, Libya the Elusive Revolution (New York: Africana Publishing, 1975), pp. 115, 265.

12. In February 1979 al-Qadhdhafi decided to change the Muslim calendar from Hijra (the Prophet's migration from Mecca to Medina, which was chosen by 'Umar Ibn al-Khattab as the date at which to begin the Muslim calendar) to the death of the Prophet in 632 AD on the grounds that the death of the last prophet was more significant than his hijra. See al-Mustaqbal 2 (March 10, 1979): 21.

13. See the pertinent observation on this matter by Michael C. Hudson, Arab Policies, the Search for Legitimacy (New Haven: Yale University Press, 1977), p. 316.

14. 'Ali 'Ali Mansur, Khutwa Ra'ida Nahwa Tatbiq Ahkam al-Shari'a al-Islamiya fi al-Jumhuriya al-'Arabiya al-Libiya (Beirut: Dar al-Fatwa, 1972), pp. 58-59, 78.

15. Ibid., pp. 66-67, 70.

16. Ibid., p. 6, for the text of the decree.

17. Ibid., pp. 6-9.

18. Ibid., p. 12.

19. Ibid., p. 72.

20. Ibid., pp. 81-82.

21. Mu'ammar al-Qadhdhafi, Al-Sijil al-Qawmi, Bayanat, wa Khutab, wa Ahadith 1970-1971, vol. 2 (n.p., n.d.), p. 117.

22. Ibid., p. 118.

23. Voll, pp. 147-48.

24. His anti-Sufi attitude has been consistent. For instance, he had the Sidi Hammuda tomb and mosque cleared from the main square of Tripoli on June 3, 1978, in spite of the strong objections of the Antiquities and Awqaf Departments. Al-Mustaqbal 2 (July 22, 1978): 17. The flocking of people to the Sidi al-Sharif tomb in mid-1980 provoked the regime to level further criticism against what it regarded as a regression to pre-Islamic practices. See Al-Zahf al-Akhdar 30 (April 4, 1980): 6-7.

25. Mu'ammar al-Qadhdhafi, Al-Sijil al-Qawmi, Bayanat, wa Khutab, wa Ahadith 1975-1976, vol. 7 (Tripoli: al-Thawra al-'Arabiya, n.d.), pp. 473-74.

26. Al-Fajr al-Jadid, February 21, 1978, p. 4.

27. Ibid., February 20, 1978, p. 3.

28. For transcendence versus immanence see Voll, pp. 147-48.

29. Al-Fajr al-Jadid, July 4, 1978, p. 4.

30. Arthur J. Arberry, The Koran Interpreted, vol. 2 (New York: Macmillan, 1955), p. 278.

31. Mu'ammar al-Qadhdhafi, Al Sijil al-Qawmi, Bayanat, wa Khutab, wa Ahadith 1974-1975, vol. 6 (Tripoli: al-Thawra al-'Arabiya, n.d.), p. 469.

32. Al-Qadhdhafi, Al-Sijil al-Qawmi, vol. 7, pp. 216-17.

33. Al-Safir, August 15, 1980, p. 9.

34. Marius K. Deeb, "Islam and Arab Nationalism in al-Qadhdhafi's Ideology," Journal of South Asian and Middle Eastern Studies 2 (Winter 1978): 14.

35. Al Qadhdhafi, Al-Sijil al-Qawmi, vol. 2, pp. 117-18.

36. Min Ahadith al-'Aqid, p. 16.

37. For a detailed exposition of al-Qadhdhafi's stand, see his speech in 'An al-Din wa-al-Qawmiya wal-Qadaya al-Muta'aliqa bihuma, 8 February 1973 (Tripoli: n.p., n.d.), pp. 14-25; Mu'ammar al-Qadhdhafi, Al-Sijil al-Qawmi, Bayanat, wa Khutab, wa Ahadith 1972-1973, vol. 4 (Tripoli: al-Thawra al-'Arabiya, n.d.), pp. 1074-75.

38. Al-Qadhdhafi, Al-Sijil al-Qawmi, vol. 7, p. 1079.

39. Al-Safir, August 15, 1980, p. 9.

40. Albert Hourani, A Vision of History, Near Eastern and Other Essays (Beirut: Khayats, 1961), p. 87.

41. Al-Safir, August 15, 1980, p. 9.

42. Ibid.

43. Ibid.

44. U.S. Department of Commerce, Office of Technical Services, Joint Publications Research Service (JPRS), Translations on Near East and North Africa, JPRS 073322, "The Religious Principles of the Ideology of al-Jamahiriya," from Al-Usbu' 'al-Siyasi, March 2, 1979, p. 14.

45. See "A Muslim Protestantism Proposed by al-Qadhdhafi," Al-Mustaqbal 2 (July 22, 1978): 17-18. We were in Libya at the time the article appeared in this Paris magazine and the issue was sold uncensored in the country, showing that that description of al-Qadhdhafi's views had at least some official approval.

Chapter 5

THE SOCIAL BASIS
OF THE REVOLUTION

SALIENT FEATURES OF THE SOCIO-
ECONOMIC STRUCTURE

A study of the social basis of the revolutionary regime in Libya
necessarily entails a brief survey of the socioeconomic structure of
Libya on the eve of the Revolution in order to comprehend the context
within which al-Qadhdhafi's ideology emerged, and the changes that
it attempted to introduce.

During the first few years of the Revolution, al-Qadhdhafi tried
to apply to Libya the social ideology of the Egyptian revolution as expounded in 'Abd al-Nasir's National Charter. However, he maintained that unlike Egypt social classes in Libya were not developed,
and class consciousness and class struggle were almost absent in
that society.[1] Was al-Qadhdhafi, as a typical nationalist leader, trying to play down class differences in Libya, or did his views reflect,
to some extent at least, the Libyan social reality?

When one examines the social structure of Libya on the eve of
the revolution two major characteristics emerge: first, the basic
socioeconomic segmentation of the society; and second, the dominant
role played by foreigners (Italians and other Europeans) and non-
Libyan Arabs (Egyptians, Palestinians, and Tunisians) in the economy
of Libya.

Concerning socioeconomic segmentation, it was only in 1963
that Libya became a unitary state in political terms. Earlier during
the monarchy it had been a federal state composed of three wilayas
(governorates), i.e., those of Tripolitania, Cyrenaica, and Fezzan.
Even under Ottoman rule the country was divided, the mutassarif
(governor) of Cyrenaica reported directly to Constantinople, as did

109

the mutassarif of Tripolitania in the latter half of the nineteenth century. Thus geopolitical segmentation was endemic in the society. Furthermore, according to Italconsult, "A large share of the country's population is still scattered in a great number of villages,"[2] and this in spite of the concentration of a large section of the population in the two main regions of Tripolitania and Cyrenaica. Due to the vastness of the desert hinterland and the rudimentary means of transport, many communities were still relatively isolated and their economic activities were confined essentially to their own region.

Misrata, a provincial town in Libya, is illustrative of some of the issues of geographical isolation and social fragmentation that are dealt with in this chapter. During the seventeenth and eighteenth centuries, the town of Misrata was an important market and caravan center dependent on transit Sahara traders. However, as those began to decline in number by the late nineteenth century, Misrata began to combine external trade, mainly through its adjacent port of Qasf Ahmad, with internal trade, serving as a commercial center for its hinterland.[3] By the first decade of this century, Misrata was trading with Malta, Benghazi, and Alexandria and the revenue of its custom house in 1902 was second to that of the custom house of the port of Tripoli itself.[4] Under Italian rule, Misrata continued to be regarded as the second city in importance in Tripolitania, although the settlers themselves did not benefit and it began to decline, continuing to do so in the post-World War II period.[5] However, with the oil boom of the 1960s, Misrata began to enjoy an unprecedented economic prosperity. And with the growing sedentarization of the nomadic and seminomadic population around it, it became an important regional commercial center again. It served a hinterland that had three kinds of land use representative of the kinds of land use in Libya as a whole. First, there was the cultivation of irrigated crops in the productive and populous region around Misrata itself. Second was the region, more sparsely populated, where the cultivation of cereals and tree crops was dependent on rainfall and did not need frequent marketing. Finally, there was the pastoral nomadism or seminomadism in the third zone, whose population infrequently used Misrata as a market center.[6]

As a market town Misrata was typical of other provincial towns in Libya with a predominance of petty traders, craftsmen, and small industrial workshops catering to its hinterland. A survey conducted in the summer of 1966 showed that there were 741 business units in Misrata, divided into 518 retail stores, 65 craftsmen workshops, 95 stall holders, and 63 light industrial enterprises.[7] Most of the trade was conducted with the hinterland, the only notable exception being the Misrata carpets that were sold beyond its hinterland and the imports of manufactured goods and processed foodstuffs that came from or via Tripoli. Misrata's fragmented and segmented petite bourgeoisie was very typical of the state of that class in the rest of Libya. In the population census of 1964, for instance, the province of Misrata had only 198 individuals categorized as employers employing others in their enterprises, and this included both urban and rural employers.[8] The total number (both urban and rural) of owners of enterprises who did not employ others was 15,801 and the total number of the economically active population of that region was 45,913.[9] The 1973 population census provides a better picture as the corresponding figures were divided into urban and rural categories. Out of a total number of 200 employers in the province of Misrata, only 31 were urban employers while the owners of business units who did not employ others numbered 1,593.[10] This clearly shows the overwhelming majority of self-employed petit-bourgeois merchants and craftsmen. Even in Libya as a whole the proportion of employers employing others did not constitute more than 6.25 percent of the total number of employers or owners of business units. In absolute numbers the figures in the 1973 census were 3,470 out of a total of 55,451 employers for Libya as a whole. Moreover, the category of owners of enterprises employing others was not divided into subcategories according to the number of employees. Therefore, one can fairly assume that a considerable proportion of the 3,470 employers did employ a small number of workers, that is, less than five workers, thus remaining within the confines of the commercial and industrial petite bourgeoisie.

If the urban socioeconomic structure is fragmented, as we have seen, the nonurban or rural and pastoral structure is equally fragmented. Historically, the Sanusiya movement emerged in a tribally based society, and the symbiosis between the Sa'adi tribes of Cyrenaica and the Sanusiya movement was almost complete. The Italians tried to settle the nomadic and seminomadic tribes and to transform collective ownership of land into individual private ownership throughout the 1930s. The British after them, however, revived tribalism and when al-Sayyid Idris established the National Congress in January 1948, it was basically tribal in character. Evans-Pritchard in his study of the Sanusi of Cyrenaica showed that the Libyan tribal structure was highly segmented: "The tribal system . . . is a system of balanced opposition between tribes and tribal sections from the largest to the smallest divisions, and there cannot therefore be any single authority in a tribe. Authority is distributed at every point of the tribal structure and political leadership is limited to situations in which a tribe or a segment of it acts corporately."[11]

The second major feature of the socioeconomic structure of Libyan urban society is the dominant role played by foreigners. Upon examining the members of the Tripoli Chamber of Commerce on the eve of the revolution one notices the predominance of non-Libyan enterprises.[12] The same is true of industrial enterprises, which totaled 189 (excluding quarries) and were licensed in accordance with the Law of Industrial Organization of 1969. The Libyan enterprises constituted a very small proportion of the total and were confined to bakeries, macaroni factories, oil presses, and the production of textiles, construction materials, soap, and paper.[13]

On the eve of the Italian occupation, Libyan traders, particularly in Tripolitania, formed a significant proportion of the community of merchants, which included foreigners and local Jews.[14] The fortunes of these Libyan merchants, with a few exceptions, were adversely affected by the Italian occupation and the Italian dominance over commerce and trade that became overwhelming by 1938.[15] The growing importance of indigenous Libyans in the economic sphere was slow in the post-World War II period, and even by the late 1960s, after the oil boom, there were relatively few. Of the old families who dealt with commerce and belonged to this class were the Bin Zikris, the Lanqis, and the 'Araqibs, who were entrepreneurs and import-export traders.[16]

Although Libya differs from other oil-exporting countries such as Kuwait, Qatar, and the Union of Arab Emirates where the nonindigenous population forms a majority, the proportion of non-Libyans among the economically active population is still sizable and was estimated in 1975 at around 30 percent of the total economically active population of Libya.[17] In fact, two-thirds of the construction workers and 40 percent of those in the manufacturing sector were non-Libyan, and in the public sector non-Libyans constituted almost 10 percent of the total number of those employed in the government service.[18] On the other hand, members of the Libyan urban middle class and of the petite bourgeoisie who were working with the government exceeded their counterparts in the private sector.[19] This dependence of the bulk of the intelligentsia and the urban middle class on the state for their employment caused the development of the indigenous private sector to trail far behind that of the public sector. This was especially the case with the unprecedented growth of the latter, occasioned first by the oil boom of the 1960s and then by the nationalization of major commercial and industrial enterprises after the revolution. An illustration of this is the proportion of the total fixed capital formation by the public sector in Libya, which was 76.9 percent to 23.1 percent for the private sector during the crucial period between 1971 and 1973.[20]

We conclude that on the eve of the revolution, in spite of the huge revenue from oil (estimated at US$1,132 million in 1969), the country had not witnessed industrialization of any consequence. No Libyan financial or industrial bourgeoisie had emerged. The only indigenous urban class of any significance was "a dispersed and fragmented commercial class that sells to the internal market,"[21] as was seen in the case of the provincial town of Misrata. Foreigners, and in particular Italians, were still dominant in the private sector of the economy.

Moreover, because of the weakness of the indigenous commercial class, the only avenue opened for the professional clerical section of the Libyan petite bourgeoisie was government service. In turn, this preponderant role of the public sector (especially with nationalization measures after the revolution) hampered the development of "a speculative and commercial bourgeoisie."[22] In the countryside, the spatial distribution of Libya's population reinforced the segmentation of the socioeconomic structure, and the tribal structure of Cyrenaica, Fezzan, and parts of Tripolitania further aggravated this problem of social fragmentation and the dispersal of political authority in Libya.

AL-QADHDHAFI'S SOCIOECONOMIC IDEAS

Al-Qadhdhafi's social, economic, and political ideology was intricately related to the salient features of the Libyan social structure. In the second chapter of his Green Book he sets forth his conception of "natural socialism" (al-ishtirakiya al-tabi'iya). In fact, he uses the term at least three times.[23] To him it is a natural socialism in three basic interrelated senses. First, it is a precapitalist form of socialism with strong anticapitalist overtones. Second, it emphasizes the egalitarianism of the new socialist order. And third, it advocates the self-sufficiency of the economic producer. Al-Qadhdhafi's conception of socialism is precapitalist in an historical manner, for it implies that "prior to the emergence of classes, forms of government and positive laws"[24] there existed a stage in history where natural socialism reigned supreme. It was a "natural" state of affairs, not unlike an idealized Lockean state of nature, where certain natural principles (qawa'id tabi'iya)[25] operated as the ultimate source of authority in defining and determining social relations in the process of production.[26] During that historical epoch there was no exploitation of man by man, and this state came about only when human society began to witness corruption and deviated from the "natural principle" of equality (al-qa'ida al-tabi'iya lil-musawat).[27] Thus, al-Qadhdhafi advocated in his Green Book the return to these "natural principles" to establish a new socialist order.[28]

This concept of equality is applied by al-Qadhdhafi to the process of production itself. He holds that there should be an equitable division of the value of manufactured goods among the three elements of production ('anasir al-intaj): the raw materials of production, the means of production, and the producer himself. Each element being "essential and necessary" in the process of production should, according to the "natural principle of equality,"[29] receive equal attention (sic!). The plausibility of this doctrine rests on al-Qadhdhafi's assumption that the three elements are equal and comparable in the first instance, and second, that although they have changed quantitatively and qualitatively over time "they did not change in their essence with respect to the role each plays in the process of production."[30]

The question arises, however, concerning the manner in which this equitable division among the three elements of production is to take place in practice. We are not enlightened on this point, although it is clear that al-Qadhdhafi wishes to abolish wage labor and make workers partners (shuraka') in the process of production. A second policy that has emerged from this theory has been the limitations placed on the amount a worker can receive as his share in the process of production, which in turn is determined by the principle of the "self-sufficiency" of the economic producer.

The self-sufficiency of the economic producer is defined in such a manner as to imply that he is engaged only in what is called a "productive activitity." The legitimate objective of an individual's economic activity is to satisfy his material needs only and not "seek profit to save over what is necessary to satisfy those needs."[31] Al-Qadhdhafi's assumption here is that there is a scarcity of economic goods in any society and that the total wealth of any society at a specific period in in time is limited. Consequently, to accumulate wealth beyond the basic necessities of life is to do so at the expense of others. The individual "has the right to save from . . . his own production but not from the work efforts of others."[32] The individual economic producer is even discouraged from becoming too economically active as that would increase his wealth beyond his needs and indirectly deprive others from satisfying their own basic needs.

Al-Qadhdhafi's belief that the individual should have his basic material needs satisfied and that clothing, food, transport, and housing are his own "personal and sacrosanct property"[33] is a reaffirmation of the ideal of the self-sufficient petit bourgeois, not unlike the prevalent type already existing in the small provincial towns of Libya. We thus find that al-Qadhdhafi's personal experience, whether in the desert or later in the provincial towns of Misrata and Sabha, molded his ideas concerning the individual economic producer. His determination to establish an egalitarian society of self-employed individuals or workers employed in public enterprises therefore comes as no surprise. Within the context of his ideas a discrepancy of wealth would be intolerable as that would lead not only to social inequalities within the society but to the accumulation of power in the hands of a few, as well, which is uncommon in a tribal society with a fragmented power structure.

Although al-Qadhdhafi denies that Marxism has had any impact on his thought he nevertheless does admit having read Marxist texts in translation and did have long discussions with Arab Marxists. When reading some of his writings and the texts of his speeches, one can detect a perceptible Marxist influence on his ideas and their expression. For instance, his depiction of the relationship between the employer and the wage laborer as quasi-slavery is not simply related to the meaning of the Arabic word ajir,[34] but is influenced by the Marxist concept of disguised exploitation in the capitalist-worker relationship. Similarly, the demand for the abolition of wage labor and the liberation of man from its oppression is an essentially Marxist idea.[35] His description of the process of change that could lead to the establishment of a new socialist order is also Marxist in terminology: "The new socialist society would be a dialectical outcome of the previously oppressive relations in the world. . . ."[36] More explicitly, al-Qadhdhafi maintains that "the transformation of the contemporary societies from societies of wage laborers to societies of partners is an inevitable and dialectical outcome of the contradicting economic theses[37] prevailing in the world today. . . ."[38] Although he does not explicitly regard the working class as the vanguard of the socialist revolution, he gives a role to the labor unions in this revolutionary transformation through their collective "threatening" power.[39] The reason for this may be found in the Libyan social structure itself, where the working class was never of any importance whether numerically or politically, Libya not having developed an industrial infrastructure of any significance.

The Marxist influence on al-Qadhdhafi's social and economic ideology was not accidental. He selected only those Marxist concepts that best fit in his egalitarian view of his society, a view rooted in the tribal nomadism of the desert and the small bourgeoisie of provincial towns.

AL-QADHDHAFI'S POLICIES IN THE SOCIOECONOMIC SPHERES

Al-Qadhdhafi's social and economic ideas neither emerged in a vacuum nor were intended as mere theorizing, but were general principles devised for political action and implementation. How did al-Qadhdhafi implement his conception of precapitalist socialism? His speech on September 1, 1978, was directed to workers in major private and public enterprises, urging them to take over the enterprises. In fact, by the end of 1978, around 180 enterprises—industrial, commercial, and others including hotels and state farms—were taken over by the workers. The workers took over the running of the enterprises and all administrative functions were under the supervision of the workers' committees. By their actions they were putting into practice al-Qadhdhafi's ideological slogan: "Partners not Wage-Laborers."[40] This was a more radical change than that advocated by the previously enacted Law of 1973, which guaranteed profit sharing for the workers if the enterprises employed more than ten workers and if their annual profit exceeded 4,000 Libyan dinars: "One fourth of the profits were to be distributed to all workers, 30 percent in cash and 70 per cent in the form of employee benefits."[41] The enterprises that were not affected by these measures were the small enterprises run by their owners or members of their families that employed few workers or non-Libyan workers. Thus we see that in practice, as in theory, al-Qadhdhafi favors the small self-employed entrepreneur. His policies are aimed at completely undermining the wealth and, consequently, much of the power of the owners, and absentee owners, of large enterprises.

In harmony with the egalitarian ethos of al-Qadhdhafi's natural socialism, the General Secretariat of the General People's Congress passed, in March 1978, Resolution No. 4, which set guidelines for the ownership of property, including the ownership of houses. The law on property ownership, which was eventually issued on May 6, 1978, stipulated that Libyan families had the right to own one house only, except in the case of widows whose only source of income was the revenue from the rent of their houses and in the case of families who had at least one son over age 18.[42] Thus families in rented houses became instant owners of their homes. The new owners, however, had to pay a mortgage in monthly installments to the government that was estimated on the basis of the income of the family. "But mortgage repayments usually amount to a third of the former rent and those with a family income of less than LD 190 pay nothing. That property, meanwhile, is deliberately undervalued for the purpose of purchase—often by as much as thirty or forty per cent."[43] The former landlords were given a compensation by the state in installments over a period of years for the appropriation of their property.[44]

The law of May 6, 1978, concerning property ownership also undermined the economic power of those who invested in real estate. In 1974, there were 3,100 house owners whose main source of revenue was rents. One can note that the absolute number of house owners who depended on rental income was small. However, the value of the fixed capital formation of house ownership increased by leaps and bounds between 1971 and the mid-1970s. In 1971 the value was estimated at 44.1 million Libyan dinars (LD), rising to 91.4 million LD in 1972 and 138.2 million LD in 1973. That year housing reached the highest proportion—20 percent—of the value of the fixed capital formation of any other economic activity in Libya. By 1974, however, it had declined slightly to 19.4 percent of the total, although the current buyers' value had gone up to 170 million LD.[45] Capital expenditure in million Libyan dinars during the period 1971-73 was 1360.1 for the whole economy, while the dwelling/building category was 277.3 million LD, constituting 20.4 percent of the total and ranking third after capital expenditure on machinery and equipment and construction, which were 22.7 percent and 21.9 percent respectively.[46]

It was not surprising, therefore, that the real estate section became by the mid-1970s the major sector of investment for Libya, especially as the regime was nationalizing industrial, financial, and commercial enterprises. As the inflow of foreign professionals and skilled laborers into Libya increased, the demand for housing pushed the prices of rents upward, and, consequently, the value of buildings for both dwelling and nondwelling purposes rose proportionately. Realizing the potential threat of the growing economic power of those urban landlords, al-Qadhdhafi issued the law of May 6, 1978, on property ownership to weaken them economically and thwart any political aspirations they may have entertained.

The law of May 6, 1978 concerning the ownership of property did not directly affect agricultural land. Agrarian reform is hardly a meaningful concept in an underpopulated society where peasants and bedouins migrate to urban centers, attracted by the opportunities made available as a result of the oil boom. The problem of the agricultural sector of Libya was just the opposite of that of Egypt, for instance. Whereas the latter's countryside was demographically saturated, in Libya there was an insufficient number of farmers to work on the available arable land.

Libya's total agricultural land amounts to 1.8 million hectares, of which 280,000 are irrigated while the rest is rainfed. However, the cropland areas shrank by 18 percent between 1960 and 1974,[47] and the agriculturally active population decreased from 145,000 in 1964 to 110,000 in 1973.[48] Individual farm owners who ran their farms as a business enterprise were very few indeed: only 453 farms had, in 1974, farm managers and 10,980 included some form of partnership in running the farms, while there were 132,952 farms that were individually owned and had an average size of 14.46 hectares.[49]

Another nonurban segment of the population that is still important, although gradually dwindling, is the nomadic and seminomadic population. It was estimated that less than 10 percent of the population in 1973 lived in tents—that is 200,000 individuals, in comparison to the estimated 320,000 who lived that way in 1964, mostly of the nomadic type. Italconsult found that "Most tent-dwellers are scattered along the Mediterranean Belt and the Steppes immediately to the South."[50] Al-Qadhdhafi himself hailed from that same region, where his family lived in a naja' (bedouin camp). His attitude toward agricultural land was, as a consequence, strongly affected by his seminomadic background. To him agricultural land belongs to God, and therefore to no one in particular. Any person has the right to cultivate the land, work on it, or graze cattle on it for his own use and that of his descendants. However, he should have no need to hire outside help. Al-Qadhdhafi, thus, undoubtedly favors the self-employed cultivator, or the shepherd-cultivator, over those who hire agricultural laborers to farm their land, an attitude similar to that he held vis-à-vis those employed in urban occupations. There is also an Islamic element present in his views toward landownership, namely, the fact that in Islamic theory and practice landownership necessarily implies its development and cultivation to justify its possession, while neglect of the land will forfeit that right of ownership. Thus ownership of land in Islam is inseparably tied to its utilization and fructification.[51] Similarly, to the tribe that is vested with tribal lands, "its soil, its arable, and its wells,"[52] landed property is not vested in any particular individual but in the community as a whole and the members are not landowners but have the right of usufruct only (al-intifa') and are called al-muntafi'un.[53] Thus here again al-Qadhdhafi's views with respect to landownership are very much a product of his tribal and Islamic background.

In our discussion of al-Qadhdhafi's conception of "natural socialism" we noted that he placed a strong emphasis on "productive" economic activity. For al-Qadhdhafi, "the one who produces is the one who consumes,"[54] which was understood to be an implied criticism of nonproductive activities, and in particular of absentee capitalists, rentiers, middlemen, and even merchants who were not involved in the process of production itself. It was feared by some to refer to trading specifically, and to its eventual elimination, as an "exploitative" and nonproductive activity.[55] Al-Qadhdhafi did maintain that profit was a manifestation of exploitation and had to be eliminated in his new socialist order. However, he also believed that this could only happen after the whole society had been transformed into a fully fledged "productive society" in which the material needs of its membergs had been satisfied and there would no longer be a need for profit.[56] Admitting that profit was the driving force behind most economic activities, and that therefore it could not be abolished by decree, al-Qadhdhafi saw the elimination of profit as "the outcome of the development of socialist production" within a particular society. Putting it paradoxically, he stated, "to work to increase profit will lead to the final disappearance of profit."[57]

If this was his official stand on profit, why then was it that by late 1978, and especially in early 1979, import trade, internal wholesale trade, and even retail trade came under such severe attack?[58] We believe that after nationalization, the taking over of the private and public enterprises by workers, and the appropriation of houses, the only economic activity left within which the private sector of the economy was still powerful was commerce. The decision to transform the economic market from an "exploitative market" into a market without merchants was aimed at undermining this last bastion of private capital, investment, and accumulation of wealth in Libyan society. [59]

In early 1979 the Libyan government abolished trade and became the sole importer in Libya, deciding on the quantity and quality of imported goods, based on the customs register as well as on the import companies' estimates of their requirements. The Economy Secretariat, however, had "the final authority in estimating their requirements" in the light of the society's real need for any commodity. [60]

It is also envisaged that the state will eventually control the marketing of agricultural produce, in part because of the Farmers' Federation's persistent complaint that individual farmers who did not market their produce through the cooperative societies or the storehouse of the Public Agricultural Production and Marketing Company fall prey to wholesale traders and middlemen. In a study on the problems facing the marketing of agricultural produce, it was pointed out that one of the problems was "the farmer's reliance on middlemen . . . and the failure of the cooperative associations to perform their desired role."[61] Subsequently, the farmer lost a large part of the returns on his produce, which were pocketed by the middlemen. Another problem that was brought up by the study concerns "the widely scattered associations and the long distances separating one from another. . . ."[62] Thus transporting the agricultural crops has proved to be a difficult problem facing the producer. This in turn has affected the consumer, who has suffered from the high retail prices. [63]

The tangible result of the campaign against trade as a profit-making institution was an increase in the shortages of the various commodities and the long queues that developed outside shops and cooperative societies. Thus the arbitrary abolition of trade did not solve, but rather created new problems for Libya. Although the decision was generally defended by partisans of the regime, they have begun having certain doubts about its efficacy, and have admitted that it failed in providing for the basic needs of the ordinary citizen. [64]

One can fairly conclude that the drive against the rentiers and real estate owners on the one hand and against wholesale traders, middlemen, and even retail traders on the other has further fragmented the already fragmented socioeconomic structure of the country. And although it has increased the number of the public sector employees, as for instance when it decided to build 158 marketplaces all over Libya, the outcome was also to create a greater measure of decentralization.

The inevitable question here is: how can such a socioeconomic system work? Paradoxically, the large revenue that the state gets from exporting oil makes it unnecessary for it to depend economically on the population, and permits al-Qadhdhafi to indulge in this vision of a precapitalist socialist society, of small self-sufficient producers whose accumulation of capital and extraction of economic surplus, whether rural or urban, is almost superfluous.

AL-QADHDHAFI'S POLITICAL IDEAS

Although al-Qadhdhafi's ideas on politics preceded his social and economic ideas, the latter was discussed first as their implementation had a greater impact on Libyan society. Furthermore, al-Qadhdhafi himself admitted that the major assumptions of his political ideas were not original. [65] His assertion, for instance, that direct democracy was the only real form of democracy was basically borrowed from Western political thinkers such as Rousseau, Robespierre, and others. [66] However, the answer to the question of why these particular ideas were selected in the first place can only be found in al-Qadhdhafi's own experience and within the context of his own society.

Al-Qadhdhafi's criticism of parliamentary democracy, the use of plebiscites, and the rule of the one-party system can be understood in his obsession with the problem of how to reconcile the representation of the whole society with the diversity that exists within a particular society. Parliamentary democracy means in effect democracy through representation , and in the Libyan context would lead, as it did during the monarchy period, to the rule of the tribal leaders and the urban notables. Thus the wealthy and the powerful would inevitably assume power in such a political system, which is unacceptable to the egalitarian and plebian instincts of al-Qadhdhafi. [67] He questions the fairness of a system in which members of parliament who constitute a tiny minority in any particular society rule in the name of the people who constitute the whole and whose active political participation is limited to the periodic exercise of their right to vote. To him that tiny minority cannot truly represent the people for whom active political participation should take place through popular congresses and popular committees only to be truly representative. Each locality, according to al-Qadhdhafi, should have a basic popular congress that in turn selects a popular committee to lead it, and in turn every basic popular committee should choose an administrative popular committee to replace the local government administration in the district. [68] This local popular committee must be, in turn, held accountable for its actions and decisions to the basic popular congress in its region.

Al-Qadhdhafi recognized as an essential part of the political system those associations that united people on the basis of their occupations or professions. Workers, peasants, students, craftsmen, and employees were encouraged to form their own unions or associations and combine membership in these organizations with membership in the popular congresses and popular committees. The leaders of the popular congresses and the popular committees and the leaders of the various labor unions have met annually since 1977 at the General People's Congress. The latter, unlike a parliament, was supposed to be the convention of the basic popular congresses, popular committees, and the various labor and professional organizations.[69] The decisions taken by the General People's Congress were then submitted to the participants to be implemented by the popular committees responsible vis-à-vis the basic popular congresses.[70]

To al-Qadhdhafi, popular democracy meant that the "sovereignty of the people is indivisible."[71] He equated political partisanship and membership in political parties with "an act of treason."[72] In the second half of the 1970s, when he felt that Libyans had become politically apathetic about participating in popular congresses and popular committees, he resorted (from 1977) to the formation of revolutionary committees (lijan thawriya) whose function it was to act as revolutionary watchdogs over the political activities of the popular committees and the secretariats of the popular congresses.[73] In effect these lijan have become extremely powerful: they can select the candidates in popular committees, can bring to trial "subversive elements," have the power of censorship, and are now publishing (since January 1980) a weekly entitled al-Zahf al-Akhdar, which propounds the regime's views. One can easily argue, consequently, that the lijan thawriya have become an undeclared political party through which the government implements and enforces its politicies.[74] This description would, however, be unacceptable to the regime, who has been traditionally against the formation of political parties, but now concedes that parties may have played a progressive role before the revolution.[75]

In conclusion we may say that behind all this rhetoric of direct democracy lies al-Qadhdhafi's basic concern to reconcile the whole society, symbolized by the General People's Congress, with its diverse and segmented parts, and by the basic popular congresses. On one level, the structure of the political system envisaged by al-Qadhdhafi is analogous to the tribal structure, with tribes and their branches being replaced by the modern structures of popular congresses and popular committees. Al-Qadhdhafi borrowed the tribal structure and adapted it to modern times without a tribal leadership, which he had done his best to undermine in the traditional structure. According to the source, "localities were divided into zones (sections) crossing old tribal boundaries, combining parts of different tribes within one zone, in an effort to destroy the power of traditional institutions and regional or local kinship."[76]

Al-Qadhdhafi's ideological symbols and analogies are also drawn from his tribal background. For instance, in his objections to party politics and to the rule of the one-party system, he maintains that the political "party is the tribe of the modern age . . . [and] that the society which is ruled by one party is exactly like a society ruled by one tribe. . . ."[77]

Over the past decade al-Qadhdhafi's social, economic, and political ideology has undergone noticeable changes. It became more radical as he attempted to move Libya further toward a system of the one-class society type.[78] Politically, an unofficial one-party system has begun to emerge in spite of his previous vehement attacks on party politics. He has also come full circle from a complete denial that social classes and class consciousness existed in Libya a decade ago to a systematic effort to obliterate existing class differences and to prevent, by any means, the emergence of class differentiation in his society. He has tried to reenact a past that he has known and experienced, while at the same time trying to forestall the future.

NOTES

1. Mu'ammar al-Qadhdhafi, Al-Sijil al-Qawmi, Bayanat, wa Khutab, wa Ahadith 1971-1972, vol. 3 (Tripoli: al-Thawra al-'Arabiya, n.d.), pp. 211-12, 342-45, 388-89.

2. Italconsult for the Government of the Libyan Arab Republic, Ministry of Planning and Scientific Research, Settlement Pattern Study, Summary (Rome, 1976), p. v.

3. Muhammad Naji and Muhammad Nur, Tarablus al-Gharb (Tripoli: Dar Maktabat al-Fikr, 1973), pp. 62, 78-81.

4. Ibid., pp. 61, 102.

5. G. H. Blake, Misurata: A Market Town in Tripolitania, Research Paper no. 9 (Durham: Department of Geography, University of Durham, 1968), p. 15.

6. Ibid., p. 22.

7. Ibid., p. 27.

8. Kingdom of Libya, Ministry of Economy and Trade, Census and Statistical Department, General Population Census, 1964 (Tripoli, n.d.), p. 32.

9. Ibid.

10. SPLAJ, Secretariat of Planning, Census and Statistics Department, Nata'ij al-Ta'dad al-'Am lil-Sukkan, 1393 AH, 1973 AD, Misrata (Tripoli: Government Press, 1977), p. 110.

11. E. E. Evans-Pritchard, The Sanusi of Cyrenaica (Oxford: Clarendon Press, 1949), p. 59.

12. Ghurfat al-Tijara wal-Sina'a, Tarablus al-Gharb, Al-Dalil al-Tijari 1968-1969 (Beirut: al-Ghuraiyib Press, 1969), pp. 251-81.

13. Ibid., pp. 315-31.

14. Ahmad Sidqi al-Dajjani, Libya Qubail al-Ihtilal al-Itali aw Trablus al-Gharb fi Akhir al-'Ahd al-'Uthmani al-Thani 1882-1911 (Cairo, 1971), p. 268.

15. Muhammad Mustafa al-Sharkasi, Lamhat 'An al-Awda' al-Iqtisadiya fi Libya Athna' al-'Ahd al-Itali (Tunis: al-'Arabiya lil-Kitab, 1976), pp. 43-44.

16. Salaheddin Hasan, "The Genesis of the Political Leadership of Libya 1952-1969: Historical Origins and Development of its Component Elements" (Ph.D. diss., George Washington University, Washington, D.C., 1973), pp. 254-66.

17. Libyan Arab Republic, Ministry of Planning and Scientific Research, Economic and Social Planning Division, Report on Economic Growth During the Period 1971-1974 (Tripoli, 1975), Table 21, p. 80.

18. Libyan Arab Republic, Ministry of Planning, "Taqrir 'an Wadi' al-Qiwa al-'Amila," mimeographed (n.p., 1974), Table 7.

19. The vast majority of the Libyans who belonged to the managerial and professional category, estimated at 11,620 in 1975, worked in the public sector. SPLAJ, Department of Information and Cultural Affairs, Facts and Figures (Tripoli, 1977), p. 156.

20. LAR, Report on Economic Growth, Table 12, p. 50.

21. Ruth First, Libya the Elusive Revolution (New York: Africana Publishing, 1975), p. 181.

22. Ibid., pp. 181, 183.

23. Mu'ammar al-Qadhdhafi, Al-Kitab al-Akhdar, al-Fasl al-Thani, Hal al-Mashkal al-Iqtisadi, al-Ishtirakiya (Tripoli: al-Sharikat al-'Amma lil-Nashr wal-Tawzi' wal-I'lan, 1977), pp. 7, 38.

24. Ibid., p. 7.

25. This term is mentioned 16 times. Ibid., pp. 7, 8, 9, 11, 13, 14, 34, 38.

26. Ibid., p. 7.

27. Ibid., p. 8.

28. Ibid., p. 7.

29. Ibid., pp. 8-11, 13.

30. Ibid., p. 10.

31. Ibid., p. 20.

32. Ibid., p. 21.

33. Ibid., p. 33.

34. Ibid., p. 4.

35. Ibid., p. 7.

36. Ibid., p. 32. The emphasis is ours.

37. The Arabic term used is al-utruhat.

38. Ibid., p. 35. The emphasis is ours.

39. Ibid.

40. Harold D. Nelson, ed., Libya a Country Study, 3d ed. (Washington, D. C.: Government Printing Office for Foreign Area Studies, The American University, 1979), p. 133; The Green March 1 (June 21, 1980): 9; see also "Workers Take over Private Sector Companies," al-Usbu' al-Siyasi, September 4, 1978, pp. 1, 2 in U.S., Department of Commerce, Office of Technical Services, Joint Publications Research Service (JPRS), Translations on Near East and North Africa, JPRS 72039, pp. 62-64. A few days after al-Qadhdhafi's speech on September 1, 1978, some 90 enterprises were taken over.

41. Nelson, p. 133.

42. The full text of the law on property ownership is in "Law on Property Ownership Published," in U.S., Department of Commerce, Office of Technical Services, JPRS 71325, pp. 80-82.

43. Jamahiriya Review 2 (July 1980): 11.

44. Nelson, p. 132.

45. LAR, Report on Economic Growth, Tables 12, p. 50; 19, p. 78; and 21, p. 80.

46. Ibid., Table 13, p. 51.

47. Italconsult, Settlement Pattern Study, Summary, p. xi.

48. Ibid.; SPLAJ, Secretariat of Planning, Census and Statistics Department, Population Census, Summary Data 1393 AH, 1973 AD (Tripoli: Government Press, n.d.), Table 22, p. 22. The 1973 figure of 110,000 workers is definitely a low estimate.

49. LAR, Maslahat al-Ihsa' wal-Ta'dad, Al-Nata'ij al-Awaliya lil-Ta'dad al-Zira'i, 1974 (Tripoli: al-'Asriya Press, 1974), pp. 1,5.

50. Italconsult, Settlement Pattern Study, Summary, p. viii.

51. "The Religious Principles of the Ideology of al-Jamahiriya," al-Usbu' al-Siyasi, March 2, 1979, p. 14, in U.S., Department of Commerce, Office of Technical Services, JPRS 73322, p. 92, see the section on landownership.

52. Evans-Pritchard, p. 55.

53. Al-Qadhdhafi, Al-Kitab al-Akhdar, al-Fasl al-Thani, p. 19.

54. Ibid., p. 4.

55. Al-Zahf al-Akhdar 1 (June 21, 1980): 11.

56. Al-Qadhdhafi, Al-Kitab al-Akhdar, al-Fasl al-Thani, pp. 36-37.

57. Ibid., p. 37.

58. Sayyid al-Jabarti, "Future Markets Without Traders," al-Usbu' al-Siyasi, January 1, 1979, pp. 20-21, in U.S., Department of Commerce, Office of Technical Services, JPRS 72901, pp. 131-34.

59. "Interview with Director General of the Economy Secretariat, Fawzi al-Shakshuki," al-Usbu' al-Siyasi, August 10, 1979, p. 3, in U.S., Department of Commerce, Office of Technical Services, JPRS 74377, pp. 34-37.

60. Ibid. The government is now building 158 marketplaces, or consumers' centers, that will be divided into three categories: five giant centers in Tripoli and Benghazi, and the other municipalities will have medium-sized and small-sized consumers' centers. According to Sayyid al-Jabarti, "One of the goals of these consumers' centers is to cut down on the huge number of merchants who are a burden on productivity. The project aims at using fewer employees with greater efficiency." U.S., Department of Commerce, JPRS 72901.

61. Sayyid al-Jabarti, "Tuesday Market: Juha's Secret-Filled House: Hundreds of Producers in Grip of Middlemen and Wholesalers," al-Usbu' al-Siyasi, August 3, 1979, pp. 4-5, in U.S., Department of Commerce, Office of Technical Services, JPRS 74316, pp. 96-101.

62. Ibid.

63. Ibid.

64. "Qarar bi I'adat al-Tijara," Al-Zahf al-Akhdar 8 (August 4, 1980): 1-2.

65. Mu'ammar al-Qadhdhafi, Al-Kitab al-Akhdar, al-Fasl al-Awal, Hal Mushkilat al-Dimuqratiya, Sultat al-Sha'b (n.p., n.d. [1976?]), pp. 28-29.

66. Al-Zahf al-Akhdar 1 (July 28, 1980): 22.

67. Al-Qadhdhafi, Al-Kitab al-Akhdar, al-Fasl al-Awal, pp. 10, 48.

68. Ibid., p. 31.

69. Ibid., pp. 32-33.

70. Ibid., p. 32.

71. Ibid., pp. 12, 17.

72. Ibid., p. 12.

73. Michel al-Nimri, "Libya fi 'Asr al-Jamahir, al-Lijan al-Thawriya, Itar al-Thawra al-Siyasiya," al-Safir, August 19, 1980, p. 11.

74. Ibid.

75. Al-Zahf al-Akhdar 1 (August 11, 1980): 24.

76. Omar el-Fathaly et al., Political Development and Bureaucracy in Libya (Lexington, Mass.: Lexington, Books, 1977), p. 39. The power of tribes in certain regions is still felt, as for instance when tribes were able to contest successfully the "elections" for the popular committees in certain areas. See the article "Role of Tribalism in al-Jamahiriyah Reviewed," al-Usbu' al-Siyasi, March 2, 1979, pp. 8-9, in U.S., Department of Commerce, Office of Technical Services, JPRS 73322, pp. 84-89.

77. Al-Qadhdhafi, Al-Kitab al-Akhdar, al-Fasl al-Awal, pp. 12, 17.

78. Al-Safir, August 15, 1980, p. 8.

Chapter 6

LIBYA'S ARAB POLICY

INTRODUCTION

The study of the foreign policy of any state should include three considerations: first, the economic and military capabilities of the state; second, its geographical and strategic position; and third, the role of the latter in regional and international politics, as conceived and practiced by its leaders.

This last chapter studies the development of Libya's foreign policy since 1969 with respect to the rest of the Arab world. Since the revolution, Libya became under al-Qadhdhafi a major participant on the Arab scene. Neither its small population, which is less than 3 million, nor its level of development, which is low, even by the standards of the rest of the Arab world, qualified Libya to play a major role. And yet the vast oil wealth that produced a surplus income (especially after the oil prices quadrupled in early 1974) has been used to further the influence of Libya in the Arab world and elsewhere. The geographical position of Libya has also been strategic in linking the Arab East (the Mashriq) with the Maghrib. Furthermore, Libya's activities acquire greater significance due to its proximity to Egypt, the most populous and most powerful of the Arab states. Additionally, the present leadership of Libya represented by al-Qadhdhafi was particularly ambitious and actively pursued the goals of its foreign policy abroad, in contrast to the more isolationist and parochial attitude of the Sanusi monarchy.

There have been four major issues with which Libyan policymakers have been concerned in their Arab policy throughout this period. In a descending order of importance, they are: the Arab-Israeli conflict, bloc formation and competition for leadership in the

Arab world, the quest for Arab unity, and finally, the support or lack of support given to revolutionary and/or liberation movements in the region.

The Arab-Israeli conflict is undoubtedly the principal issue that has, to a large extent, determined Libya's Arab policy during the period under study. Libya's position on some of the basic landmarks of the conflict, such as the U.N. Resolution 242 of November 1967, the October War of 1973, the step-by-step Kissinger diplomacy, and the Camp David Agreements that resulted in the normalization of relations between Egypt and Israel, will be examined in this chapter in addition to its relations with the Palestinian Liberation Organization (PLO) and its various member organizations.

Bloc formation in the Arab world is the second most important issue, involving Libya's relations with the major Arab powers, especially those vying for political leadership on the regional level, and superpowers, who played a role in promoting or at least supporting the formation of regional blocs or alliances.

Arab unity is the third issue of major concern to foreign-policy makers in Libya to which al-Qadhdhafi was always sympathetic since his youth, when he listened to that powerful source of political socialization of the late 1950s and the 1960s, the Voice of the Arabs broadcast from Cairo.[1] Libya's historical divisions into Tripolitania, Cyrenaica, and Fezzan, and consequently the lack of a clearly defined Libyan identity, pushed al-Qadhdhafi to go beyond his own borders, to week a wider identity in Arab unity.

The fourth major issue of Libya's Arab policy is its support for liberation and/or revolutionary movements in the Arab world. Libya's stand on this issue has changed considerably over the last decade, but its interest in such movements has remained wide, encompassing the entire scope of the Arab world from the Western Sahara in northwestern Africa to 'Uman in the Gulf.

The importance of, and the priority given to, these issues by Libya has varied from one period to another. We have consequently divided the 11 years since the revolution into four periods demarcated by important regional events or series of events in order to understand more clearly and discern meaningful patterns in Libya's Arab foreign policy since 1969.

The first period is short in duration, and extends from September 1, 1969, when al-Qadhdhafi came to power, to the end of 1970, which is demarcated by Egyptian President 'Abd al-Nasir's death on September 28, 1970. During that period, the war of attrition on the Suez Canal was still raging and Palestinian guerrillas were still active on the Jordanian front, and therefore the Arab-Israeli conflict loomed large in the minds of the Libyan leaders. Another issue in which al-Qadhdhafi showed interest during that period was Arab unity under the aegis of Nasir himself. This implied some form of bloc formation led by Egypt, although unimportant at that time as the Arab world was not yet polarized politically. Libya's support for liberation and revolutionary movements except for the Palestinian guerrillas, was minimal during that period.

The second period extended from January 1971, with the formation of the Federation of Arab Republics (FAR), including Egypt, Syria, and Libya, and lasted until the eve of the Arab-Israeli War of October 1973. The war put an end to Libya's obsession with Arab unity, first through the FAR and then with Egypt, between February 1972 and September 1973. Priority was given to the Arab-Israeli conflict during those two years, which were also marked by the successful attempt by King Husain to oust the Palestinian guerrillas from Jordan. Polarization of the Arab countries and bloc formation were not yet clear during that period. Libya's support for liberation and revolutionary movements was confined to some Palestinian guerrilla organizations like the Fath and to moral support for antimonarchical movements, such as those that attempted the coups of July 1971 and August 1972 against King Hasan II of Morocco.

The third period, which began with the outbreak of the October War of 1973, was marked by a sense of unity and common purpose among the Arab countries that gradually and steadily eroded, especially with the signing of the Second Sinai Agreement in September 1975. The attitude toward the peaceful settlement of the Arab-Israeli conflict led to greater polarization, and signs of bloc formation in the Arab world emerged. Libya, in particular, became actively involved in the support of liberation and revolutionary movements, whether within the ranks of the PLO or the Lebanese National Movement, during the civil war of 1975-76. After the abortive union with Tunisia in January 1974, Libya steered away from any further attempt at Arab unity. The relations with Egypt had its ups and downs, and eventually broke down into open conflict and confrontation in the border war between the two countries in July 1977. This period ends on the eve of Sadat's historic visit to Jerusalem.

The fourth period began with Sadat's visit to Jerusalem on November 19, 1977. The impact of the visit had tremendous repercussions on Libya's Arab foreign policy. The Arab-Israeli conflict became the single most important issue determining its foreign policy toward other Arab countries. It led al-Qadhdhafi to establish an anti-Egyptian regional bloc in December 1977 with Syria, Algeria, South Yemen, and the PLO that was called the Front of Steadfastness and Confrontation (Jabhat al-Sumud wal-Tasaddi). Bloc formation became a means for him with which to challenge Sadat's action, a means he continued using throughout the period of negotiations of the Camp David Agreements and until the signature in March 1979 of the Egyptian-

Israeli Peace Treaty. Libya also continued to support liberation and
revolutionary movements during that period, but with much less enthusiasm as realism on one hand and the fear of Egypt on the other
began to have their effect. Arab unity, the attempted Libyan merger
with Syria in September 1980 notwithstanding, became the least of
Libya's concerns from November 1977.

LIBYA'S ARAB POLICY FROM SEPTEMBER 1969
TO DECEMBER 1970

The September 1, 1969, revolution in Libya took place in the
midst of a period of revolutionary upheavals that immediately followed
the Arab defeat in the June War of 1967. One of the major developments
that characterized that period was the rise of the Palestinian guerrilla
movement both as a substitute for the defeated regular Arab armies
and as a peculiarly Palestinian reaction to the Arabs' inability to meet
the Israeli challenge. Another development that had taken place on
May 25, 1969, was the military coup in Sudan led by Ja'far al-Numairi,
which drew that country closer to Nasir's Egypt. Thus when the coup
led by al-Qadhdhafi took place in Libya, it was a culmination of this
revolutionary upheaval. Al-Qadhdhafi looked up to Nasir as the leading
figure in the Arab world. As long as the war of attrition was going on
in the Suez Canal area and the Palestianian Resistance Movement
(PRM) was active across the Jordan river and Southern Lebanon, the
Arab-Israeli conflict remained the first priority for the new Libyan
regime. As early as September 1969 a committee was formed in Libya
to collect donations to be given to the Fath Palestinian guerrilla
organization. It also called for an emergency Arab League meeting to
discuss the clashes between the PRM and the Lebanese Army in October 1969. Al-Qadhdhafi sent a message to Lebanese President Charles
Hilu expressing his concern about these incidents. In fact, Libya supported Egyptian mediators, who were able to assist the two sides in
settling their differences, a settlement that was formalized in what
came to be known as the Cairo Agreement. After al-Qadhdhafi's visit
to Lebanon in June 1970, he continued his policy of mediation between
the two sides. Meanwhile, some clashes had already taken place between the Palestinian guerrillas and the Jordanian Army in February
1970 and Libya again took a stand, criticizing Jordan's attempt to
restrict the activities of the PRM and expressing its full support for
the latter.

The September crisis of 1970 in Jordan greatly preoccupied the
Libyan government. It sided with the PRM and officially stopped economic aid to Jordan as part of the financial support for confrontation
states that bordered with Israel, agreed upon in the Khartoum Arab

Summit of August 1967. After an attempt to mediate between the two
sides failed, Libya decided on September 26, 1970, not only to cut off
all aid to Jordan, but also to break off diplomatic relations with that
country.

Closely linked to his support of the PRM was the attempt on the
part of al-Qadhdhafi to unite the efforts of the Arab countries in their
struggle against Israel. On May 15, 1970, he called for the pan-Arabization of the struggle (qawmiyat al-ma'raka) and asked all Arab countries that had the means to pool their funds in order to finance the war
effort against Israel. He demanded specific financial and military con-
tributions, relying primarily on the oil-producing countries as well
as on those that could send military troops. The rulers of five Arab
countries, namely, Egypt, Syria, Iraq, Jordan, and Libya, and rep-
resentatives of Sudan and Algeria met in Tripoli in June 1970, and
decided on a pan-Arab plan against Israel. They also decided that there
should be a military conference to assess the situation in terms of
what was needed for this purpose. In fact, a conference of the Minis-
ters of Foreign Affairs and Defence was convened in Tripoli on August
15 and 16 of that year, where Egypt, Syria, Libya, Sudan, and Jordan
were represented. They drafted a proposal that included specific demands in terms of troops and money to be met by some of the Arab
countries represented at the meeting in an attempt to coordinate their
military efforts against Israel. However, the acceptance of Egypt and
Jordan of the Rogers Plan for a cease-fire in August 1970 dealt a
heavy blow to the effort that had been made to establish a unified Arab
military strategy against Israel. Iraq and Algeria opted out of the agreement on the grounds that any peaceful settlement ruled out military
confrontation with Israel, and consequently any need for a unified military front as well.

During the first period extending from September 1969 to December 1970, Libya's Arab policy was in its formative stage. Although
the charismatic leadership of Nasir, whom the Libyan revolutionaries
looked up to, dominated the scene, nevertheless, it was Libya who
took the initiative in setting forth the plan for the pan-Arabization of
the struggle against Israel. Moreover, despite the fact that Libya's
efforts were being exerted domestically to remove all foreign military
bases, in particular British and American bases, from Libya, an
evacuation of which took place in March and June 1970, respectively,
al-Qadhdhafi remained actively involved in inter-Arab politics, and
on several occasions personally visited Egypt, Sudan, Iraq, Syria,
Jordan, and Lebanon.

This period also witnessed the emergence of a nucleus of progressive Arab countries led by Egypt, which was encouraged by the
revolutionary changes taking place in Sudan and Libya in 1969. Diver-
gent views were clearly voiced in the Rabat Arab Summit of December

1969, reminiscent of the polarization between progressive and conservative regimes prior to 1967. On the heels of the Rabat summit, Nasir of Egypt, Al-Numairi of Sudan, and al-Qadhdhafi of Libya signed a common declaration for cooperation known later as the Tripoli Pact, and planned to convene periodically at summit conferences.[2] There was evidence that Nasir was showing signs, in the last year of his life, of a renewal of faith in his capacity to influence events, whether by creating a new revolutionary bloc or by being amenable to overtures from the United States for a peaceful settlement of the Middle East conflict. Libya during that period worked closely and toed the line behind Egypt, the major Arab state on its eastern border, and its major geopolitical interest remained within the confines of the Arab East.

LIBYA'S ARAB POLICY DURING THE PERIOD FROM JANUARY 1971 TO SEPTEMBER 1973

The most characteristic feature of the period from January 1971 to September 1973 was Libya's quest for Arab unity. For domestic as well as for inter-Arab reasons, Syria's new regime, under Hafiz Asad, and Egypt under the new president, Anwar al-Sadat, were both interested in taking a modest step toward Arab unity. The ideal of the young revolutionary leaders of Libya since they took power had been Arab unity, and consequently, they enthusiastically joined Egypt and Syria in forming on April 17, 1971, the Federation of Arab Republics (FAR). The talks that led to the Benghazi Declaration announcing the formation of the FAR were tense. Syria wanted a federation as the first stage toward unity. The Egyptian leaders were divided: 'Ali Sabri was more enthusiastic about a union with Libya, while Sadat endorsed the Syrian viewpoint and was in favor of a federation. Al-Qadhdhafi, on the other hand, wanted an integrative type of unity among the three countries.[3] The FAR was a loose federation, which compared with the United Arab Republic (the union of Egypt and Syria between 1958 and September 1961) was a very modest undertaking indeed. Less than a year later, Libya took the initiative in demanding in February 1972 an immediate and integrative unity between Egypt and Libya. Sadat studied Libya's proposal, and on August 2, 1972, the Tubroq-Benghazi Declaration was issued in which the two countries agreed to unite, forming a unified political command and setting up seven joint committees to lay the foundations for unity in various areas such as constitutional matters, political organizations, defense, economic systems, and so forth. The deadline for the realization of this merger between Libya and Egypt was set for September 1, 1973.

In spite of the numerous meetings of the joint Egyptian-Libyan committees it became clear that the two countries were gradually moving apart. Because al-Qadhdhafi was insisting on a popular revolution and on adherence to Islamic shari'a as the source of legislation, the gulf between Libya and Egypt was widening. In order to force the hand of Sadat, al-Qadhdhafi organized a march on July 18, 1973, from Ra's Jabir, the westernmost point on the Libyan border, to Cairo.[4] The Libyans reached Cairo on July 21, 1973, and the representative of the marchers submitted a document demanding the complete and integrative unity of Libya and Egypt. Thus the period between January 1971 and September 1973 was characterized by Libya's obsession with Arab unity, an ideal that failed to materialize in the cases of both the FAR, which al-Qadhdhafi described as a "nominal federation,"[5] and the merger with Egypt.

The Arab-Israeli conflict during the same period was in a state of neither peace nor war, preceding as it did the October War of 1973. The conflict had become of secondary importance to Libya, especially as the cease-fire on the Suez Canal was holding and the Jordanian front was silent after the expulsion of the Palestinian guerrillas in the summer of 1971. Al-Qadhdhafi continued to support the PRM, primarily the Fath and the Popular Front for the Liberation of Palestine-General Command (PFLP-GC), but not those he referred to as "ideological organizations," such as the Popular Front for the Liberation of Palestine (PFLP) and the Popular Democratic Front for the Liberation of Palestine (PDFLP).

Libya regarded itself as "progressive" (taqaddumi), meaning that it supported coups or revolutions against traditional and/or monarchic regimes, a hangover from the Nasserite era of the 1960s, although it did not support all coups in the Arab world. During this period, for instance, it called for the overthrow of King Husain of Jordan, especially after his liquidation of the PRM from Jordan. Similarly, al-Qadhdhafi gave both his moral and verbal support to the attempted coups of July 1971 and August 1972 against King Hasan II of Morocco. On the other hand, when an abortive leftist coup took place in July 1971 in the Sudan, supported by the Sudanese Communist Party, Libya condemned it and returned two top leaders of the coup who were forced to land in Libya to the Sudan to be executed by al-Numairi.

During that same period regional alliances and blocs were almost absent on the Arab scene, as the FAR was not a serious federation at all. Moreover, the Sadat-Asad-Faisal axis that emerged prior, and in preparation, to the October War of 1973 defied any kind of ideological categorization as a regional bloc. Libya, on the other hand, tried to come to terms with the new leaders of Egypt and Syria and with an Arab world without Nasir, but failed to realize any of its dreams of integrative unity with either the whole or even part of the region.

LIBYA'S ARAB POLICY FROM
OCTOBER 1973 TO OCTOBER 1977

The October War was a very important watershed with respect
to Libya's Arab policy. The Arab-Israeli conflict came up so dramat-
ically to the forefront that it overshadowed the three other issues.
Arab unity, that mystical quest of al-Qadhdhafi's, produced yet another
union, this time with Tunisia. The Arab Islamic Republic was declared
on the island of Jirba on January 12, 1974, by Bourguiba and al-
Qadhdhafi, but was very short-lived. It was a sign of Libya's frustra-
tion with efforts at unity in the Arab East that it was now turning to
its Maghrebi neighbors. As early as September 1973, al-Qadhdhafi
had already proposed a union of the countries of the Maghreb, excluding Morocco, in the wake of the failure of Libya's merger with Egypt.

The October War of 1973 united the Arab countries in a moment
of enthusiasm, and for almost two years the euphoria of the war kept
the Arab world in an unprecedented state of harmony and cooperation,
without any significant polarization or bloc formation. However, this
did not augur well for Libya. Already before the Arab-Israeli war of
October 1973, the relationship between Egypt and Libya had shown
signs of strain. The fact that al-Qadhdhafi was not consulted and therefore did not participate in the decision to launch the October 6 attack
against Israeli forces in Sinai and the Golan Heights further estranged
him from Sadat, Asad, and the other Arab leaders. [6] He felt he had
been slighted and regarded only as a junior partner of the FAR. Neither
Libya's army nor its arsenal (except perhaps for the French Mirage
planes) had qualified him to be on equal footing with the other major
Arab countries represented in the FAR. This infuriated al-Qadhdhafi,
and probably determined to a large extent his attitude toward the
October War of 1973 and toward Egypt in particular for a long time
afterward. Moreover, the war had increased, in the eyes of the people
and rulers of the Arab world, the prestige of Sadat and Asad, and even
that of King Faisal of Saudi Arabia. Al-Qadhdhafi had been left out in
the cold, and could hardly claim, with any credibility, that he had
played any role in that war. His desire to be treated on par with Sadat
and Asad had been thwarted, as their newly acquired charisma put
al-Qadhdhafi in a position inferior to theirs.

It can be argued, with some measure of plausibility, that al-
Qadhdhafi's attitude toward the Arab-Israeli conflict has been very
different from that of Sadat, even during the period 1973-77. This was
due in part to al-Qadhdhafi's attitude, which was consistently against
any peaceful settlement of the conflict. He opposed the U.N. Resolution 242 of November 1967, supported the idea of an Arab Palestine
where only those indigenous Jews who had lived there during the
British Mandate would be incorporated in this state, [7] and did not

approve of the idea of a Palestinian state on the West Bank and the Gaza strip as the solution to the Palestinian problem. Libya could well afford to be rejectionist and against any settlement of the conflict because unlike Egypt, Jordan, Syria, and Lebanon it had no common border with Israel. Geographical proximity to, or distance from, Israel has always been an important element in determining the attitude of the Arab countries to that state. Furthermore, al-Qadhdhafi frequently urged the Palestinians to form a government in exile, a proposition that was anathema to some of the more radical Palestinian organizations, such as George Habash's PFLP.[8] However, on other occasions, in a more conciliatory frame of mind, he maintained that the Palestinians had the right to negotiate with the Israelis in a Geneva-type Middle East conference under the auspices of the United Nations.[9] More significantly perhaps was the fact that Libya before and after the October War of 1973 allied itself to countries that accepted the U.N. Resolution 242 of November 1967, such as Egypt under Nasir and Syria under Asad. Consequently, his stand on the Arab-Israeli conflict was not really the bone of contention between Sadat and al-Qadhdhafi during the period 1973-77. In examining the matter more closely one could discern two basic reasons for the Qadhdhafi-Sadat rift: first, Libya's ambition to play a greater role in Arab politics than its actual military, political, and demographic capabilities would allow it to. Al-Qadhdhafi always wanted Libya to be regarded and accepted by other major Arab states as a major and pivotal actor on the Arab scene. Second, al-Qadhdhafi's attempt to establish a special relationship between Libya and Egypt similar to the one it had during 'Abd al-Nasir's rule. Sadat, however, did not take either of these two aspirations very seriously. The outcome was an ambivalent love/hate relationship between Libya and Egypt. Subsequently, al-Qadhdhafi felt that "the two countries should either united or be on a collision course,"[10] a state of affairs reminiscent of the unity attempts prior to 1973 and predicting the conflict between the two nations in the post-October War period that culminated in the border war of July 1977.

Al-Qadhdhafi realized, especially since October 1973, that Libya was not being taken seriously, inter alia, because of its weak military capability, and so he embarked on an armament program. Ironically the war, which Libya had not been particularly enthusiastic about, led to the quadrupling of the price of oil, and the Libyan revenue from oil soared from approximately US$1.5 billion in 1972 to US$6.6 billion in 1974.[11] As a result, al-Qadhdhafi could easily afford sophisticated arms, which he tried to buy from both Western Europe and, more significantly, from the Soviet Union. As Egypt moved closer to the West, with Kissinger's shuttle diplomacy and the Egyptian-Israeli disengagement agreements of February 1974 and September 1975, culminating in the abrogation of the Egyptian-Soviet Treaty of Friendship

in May 1976, Libya moved in the opposite direction, closer to the
Soviet Union. Libyan Prime Minister Abd al-Salam Jallud's visit to
the Soviet Union in May 1974 took place in order to explore the domain
of the common interest of both countries, and a modest arms deal was
concluded. Aleksei Kosygin's visit to Libya in May 1975 led to greater
cooperation between the two countries and the sale of a larger arms
deal. Finally, al-Qadhdhafi's first visit to Moscow in December 1976
cemented the Libyan-Soviet relations. If the "collision course" was
unavoidable between Libya and Egypt, as al-Qadhdhafi seemed to
think, then the different parts of the jigsaw puzzle would fall into place
in a meaningful pattern. The Soviet Union had found a substitute for
Egypt on the Mediterranean coast of North Africa, and Libya had as
the main source of its arms supply the Soviet Union, which was also
ready to train its armed forces. Although, as some have pointed out,
Libya's arsenal could not be used by Syria and the PLO against Israel,
it was nonetheless primarily to upgrade its own military capability in
order to acquire more credibility as a major power in its own right
in the Arab world and in order to protect itself from a potential military threat from Egypt that Libya acquired that arsenal of weapons.
Paradoxically, the closer the Libyan ties with the Soviet Union became,
the more legitimate appeared Sadat's claim in the eyes of the United
States that Egypt was the bulwark against Soviet expansionism in the
Middle East and Africa.

Libya's attempt at bloc formation with other Arab countries
during the period 1973-77 did not succeed. An attempt in June 1975
to establish a unified military front including Syria, Iraq, and the PLO
did not materialize either, as the Lebanese Civil War intervened and
Saudi Arabia viewed Libya's role with suspicion. During the later
stages of the Lebanese war, Libya busied itself mediating between the
PLO and Syria. Later, when the six-nation summit in Riyad put an
end to the Lebanese Civil War, Jallud claimed it was Libya's efforts
that had diffused the situation, [12] and consequently that it had played
a more important role than Saudi Arabia—an attempt at enhancing
Libya's image as a major Arab power. One of the by-products of the
Saudi efforts to put an end to the Lebanese Civil War was an Egyptian-
Syrian reconciliation. This worried Libya, who had wished to have
Egypt isolated from the rest of the Arab world in order to thrive as
the spearhead of an anti-Egyptian and antisettlement movement. However, during that period the formation of an alliance against Egypt
was unthinkable, so Libya began instead to improve its relations with
Egypt after the border war of July 1977 during the months of September
and October 1977. Sadat's visit to Jerusalem on November 19, 1977,
put an abrupt end to these efforts. His historic visit changed the character of inter-Arab relations and Libya entered a new phase in its
Arab policy.

Finally, during the period 1975-77 Libya's aid to liberation and radical movements increased as its foreign policy in general moved more toward the Left. It expressed strong support in February 1975 for the Dhufar revolutionaries who were against Sultan Qabus of 'Uman, and also supported the Algerians on the Sahara question. In Lebanon, Libya aided the Lebanese National Movement throughout the Lebanese Civil War and developed new ties with the radical members of the Palestinian Resistance Movement, boasting all the while that it was the only country which supported the "rejectionists" in the Arab world.[13]

LIBYA'S ARAB POLICY FROM
NOVEMBER 1977 TO SEPTEMBER 1980

Sadat's visit to Jerusalem on November 19, 1977, led to the formation of the Steadfastness and Confrontation Front (SCF), Jabhat al-Sumud wal-Tasaddi, which was convened during December 2-5, 1977, in Tripoli, including as members Syria, Algeria, Libya, South Yemen, and the PLO. Iraq attended the conference but refused to sign the official declaration after disagreeing with Syria. Libya played an important role in the formation of the SCF, and in a way fulfilled its longtime objective of creating an anti-Egyptian front. The SCF supported important revolutionary and liberation movements in the Arab world. The Dhufar revolutionaries, for instance, were supported by the SCF because of the participation of South Yemen in the Front as was the POLISARIO because of Algeria's membership in the Front. The Palestinians were of course represented by the major organizations of the PLO in the SCF itself. Libya's activism in the Arab world increased and since November 1977 its aspirations to play a major role in Arab politics were to some extent realized. In the wake of Sadat's visit to Jerusalem, Libya convened a permanent congress of parties and organizations from all Arab countries that opposed Sadat's policies—another instrument, on the popular level, that al-Qadhdhafi used to further his influence in the region.

Opposition to Sadat's peace initiative, the Camp David Agreements, and the Israeli-Egyptian Peace Treaty went beyond the confines of the SCF. This very fact weakened the Front, which did not include such major Arab powers as Saudi Arabia, Iraq, and Morocco. The first two, in particular, were strongly opposed to Sadat's policies. Egypt, in fact, had only the support of three other states of the 22-member Arab League, namely, Sudan, 'Uman, and Somalia. Consequently, the Arab League itself, whose headquarters were moved from Cairo to Tunis (after March 1979) became a major vehicle against Sadat's peace agreement with Israel. Libya, therefore, to gain greater support against Sadat, had to alter its Arab foreign policy in two basic ways. First, it had to mend its bridges with as many Arab countries as possible, and al-Qadhdhafi himself in June 1979 (after the signing of the Egyptian-Israeli Peace Treaty on March 26, 1979) visited Syria, Jordan, Iraq, Kuwait, Bahrain, Qatar, the United Arab Emirates, Saudi Arabia, North Yemen, and South Yemen. Second, Libya had to change its stand on the Arab-Israeli conflict. Neither the SCF as such nor the Arab League's opposition to Sadat's peace treaty with Israel were against a peaceful settlement of the conflict—what they were objecting to was the separate peace treaty and the way in which the national rights of the Palestinian people and their right to establish an independent sovereign state had been virtually ignored. Thus Libya, reluctantly, moved further away from its previously held "rejectionist" stand.

Arab unity, as an issue, did not loom large during that period. Al-Qadhdhafi, however, called occasionally for regional unification, whether of the states of the Maghreb or of those of Greater Syria. In September 1980, to the surprise of many, he called for a merger with Syria, to which the latter responded favorably. The union resulted only in more economic and military aid to Syria and stronger political ties between the two countries.

CONCLUSION

In conclusion we can trace three predominant patterns in Libya's relations with other Arab countries. As we have shown, Libya has often been in political conflict with its Arab neighbors. However, it could not be on bad terms with all the major Arab powers simultaneously. Thus while Libyan-Egyptian relations were steadily deteriorating from early 1975 until the culmination of the conflict in the Libyan-Egyptian border war of July 1977, al-Qadhdhafi sought to improve his relations with other Arab countries, especially with Egypt's potential rivals in the region. Second, Libya has tended to antagonize its bordering Arab states, namely Egypt, Sudan, Tunisia, and Algeria, to a greater degree than other states, but never all four at the same time. Al-Qadhdhafi has tended to quarrel primarily with the major Arab powers such as Egypt, Saudi Arabia, Syria, Iraq, Algeria, and Morocco rather than with the minor ones, unless those had common borders with Libya. A third discernible pattern has been al-Qadhdhafi's basic antagonism toward the more conservative states in the Arab world ruled by monarchs because he felt a greater affinity for republican regimes ruled by military officers.

Nevertheless, in general, al-Qadhdhafi has shown some pragmatism in his dealings with other Arab countries. He has been able to put an end to a dispute as quickly as he was capable of starting a new one. His tribal background was undoubtedly a major factor in enabling him to reconcile himself so easily with his adversaries. The volatility of his Arab policy, however, has hampered the establishment of stable relations[14] with almost all the major Arab powers. When alliances were made, or regional blocs formed, Libya's participation was hardly ever a source of stability. A very good example of al-Qadhdhafi's Arab foreign policy is seen in Libya's relations with Egypt, which deteriorated in March 1976 when al-Qadhdhafi claimed that he could topple the Egyptian regime and even called for a popular uprising in May 1976. However, as an Egyptian-Saudi-Sudanese alliance emerged with clear anti-Libyan intentions during the summer of 1976 and an imminent reconciliation was in the offing between Egypt and Syria in a projected Arab summit in October of that year, al-Qadhdhafi began in September 1976 to speak of reaching an understanding with Egypt and even proposed meeting with Sadat. Libya sought to improve its relations with Egypt through the mediation of the PLO in the wake of the six-leader Arab summit in Riyad, and later that same month at the Arab summit in Cairo. Libyan-Egyptian relations had reached a very low point between February and May 1977, and it was becoming apparent that Egypt was preparing a punitive military attack against Libya. Al-Qadhdhafi, fearing his formidable neighbor on his eastern border, called for an Arab summit conference on June 11, 1977, to be held in Tripoli and hurriedly sent his foreign minister on a tour of 15 Arab countries during the second half of June 1977, an itinerary that included the major Arab countries, Syria, Iraq, Saudi Arabia, Algeria, and Morocco. Al-Qadhdhafi hoped that an Arab summit held in his capital would ward off an imminent Egyptian attack. Although the Libyan-Egyptian border war of July 1977 did take place and the proposed Arab summit did not, Arab mediators—particularly Algerian President Hawari Boumediene and the PLO Chief Yasir 'Arafat—were instrumental in putting an end to the conflict.

NOTES

1. This influence was so tremendous that al-Qadhdhafi decided to adopt the tune that preceded the news bulletin of the Voice of the Arabs broadcast as Libya's national anthem!

2. Mu'ammar al-Qadhdhafi, Thawrat al-Sha'b al-Libi, vol. 1 (Benghazi, 1972), pp. 389-90.

3. For the Libyan point of view see 'Abd al-Wahhab Muhammad al-Zantani, La Watha'iq October bal Watha'iq al-Wahda (Benghazi, n.d.), p. 37.

4. Mu'ammar al-Qadhdhafi, Al-Sijil al-Qawmi, Bayanat, wa Khutab, wa Ahadith 1972-1973, vol. 4 (Tripoli: al-Thawra al-'Arabiya, n.d.), pp. 1291-92.

5. Mu'ammar al-Qadhdhafi, Min Ahadith al-'Aqid Mu'ammar al-Qadhdhafi fi al-Sahafa al-'Arabiya wal-'Alamiya, from August 2, 1973 to April 29, 1974 (Tripoli: al-Thawra al-'Arabiya, n.d.), p. 110.

6. Ibid., p. 45.

7. Ibid., pp. 47, 59, 102.

8. See, for instance, Arab Report and Record 11 (May 16-31, 1978): 313.

9. Arab Report and Record 8 (February 15-28, 1975): 146.

10. Al-Qadhdhafi, Min Ahadith al-'Aqid, p. 122.

11. Wilfrid Knapp, North West Africa: a Political and Economic Survey, 3d ed. (Oxford: Oxford University Press, 1977), p. 213.

12. Arab Report and Record 9 (November 16-30, 1976): 699.

13. Arab Report and Record 9 (May 1-15, 1976): 289.

14. Knapp, p. 228.

BIBLIOGRAPHY

BOOKS AND ARTICLES

Allan, J. A., K. S. Mclachlan et al., eds. Libya: Agriculture and Economic Development. London: Frank Cass, 1973.

Arberry, Arthur J. The Koran Interpreted. Vol. 2. New York: Macmillan, 1955.

Ashiurakis, Ahmed. About Libya. Tripoli: Dar al-Farjani, 1973.

Attir, Mustafa O. "Attitudes Towards Modernization in Libya." Pilot Study. University Center for Urban Research, University of Pittsburgh, July 1977.

Blake, G. H. Misurata: A Market Town in Tripolitania. Research Paper no. 9. Durham: Department of Geography, University of Durham, 1968.

Brown, L. Carl. "The Sudanese Mahdiya." In Protest and Power in Black Africa, edited by Robert I. Rotberg and Ali A. Mazrui. New York: Oxford University Press, 1970.

Al-Dajjani, Ahmad Sidqi. Libya Qubail al-Ihtilal al-Itali aw Tarablus al-Gharb fi Akhir al-'Ahd al-'Uthmani al-Thani 1882-1911. Cairo, 1971.

Deeb, Marius K. "Islam and Arab Nationalism in al-Qadhdhafi's Ideology." Journal of South Asian and Middle Eastern Studies 2 (Winter 1978): 12-26.

Evans-Pritchard, E. E. The Sanusi of Cyrenaica. Oxford: Clarendon Press, 1949.

al-Fahoum, Siba. La Femme Lybienne en Dix Ans 1965-1975. Beirut: The Lebanese Branch of the World Feminine League for Peace and Freedom, n.d.

el-Fathaly, Omar I. "The Prospects of Public Political Participation in Libyan Local Government." Ph.D. dissertation, Department of Government, Florida State University, 1975.

el-Fathaly, Omar I., et al. Political Development and Bureaucracy in Libya. Lexington, Mass.: Lexington Books, 1977.

al-Fenaish, Ahmed Ali. "Developing an Educational Guidance Program for Libya." University of Libya, Bulletin of the Faculty of Education 2 (1971): 5.

al-Fenaish, Ali. Al-Mujtama' al-Libi wa Mushkilatihi. Tripoli, 1967.

First, Ruth. Libya the Elusive Revolution. New York: Africana Publishing, 1975.

Habib, Henri. Politics and Government of Revolutionary Libya. Ottawa: Le Cercle du Livre de France, 1975.

Hall, Peter. The World Cities. New York: McGraw-Hill, 1971.

Hasan, Salaheddin. "The Genesis of the Political Leadership of Libya 1952-1969: Historical Origins and Development of its Component Elements." Ph.D. dissertation, George Washington University, Washington, D.C., 1973.

"Hatta la Nasil ila al-Tariq al-Masdud." Al-Bayt 13 (October 5, 1977): 32.

Hilal, Jamil. Dirasat fi al-Waqi' al-Libi. Tripoli: Maktabat al-Fikr, n.d.

Hourani, Albert. A Vision of History, Near Eastern and Other Essays. Beirut: Khayats, 1961.

Hudson, Michael C. Arab Politics, the Search for Legitimacy. New Haven: Yale University Press, 1977.

"Ikhtitam A'mal al-Multaqa al-Awal lil-Lijan al-Thawriya al-Nisa'iya bi-Hay al-Andalus." Al-Zahf al-Akhdar 1 (August 11, 1980): 14.

International Bank for Reconstruction and Development. The Economic Development of Libya. Baltimore: Johns Hopkins Press, 1960.

International Labor Office. "Demographic Trends in Libya 1954-1968." Project of Planning and Evaluation of the Workforce in Libya. Mimeographed. Tripoli, 1968.

Italconsult, for the Libyan Arab Republic, Ministry of Planning and Scientific Resarch. Settlement Pattern Study, Appendix. Rome, 1976.

_____. Settlement Pattern Study, Gharyan Region. Rome, 1976.

_____. Settlement Pattern Study, National Report. Rome, 1976.

_____. Settlement Pattern Study, Summary. Rome, 1976.

_____. Settlement Pattern Study, Tripoli Region. Rome, 1976.

al-Kabir, Yassin Ali. "Assimilation of Rural Migrants in Tripoli, Libya." Ph.D. dissertation, Department of Sociology, Case Western University, Cleveland, January 1972.

Khadduri, Majid. Modern Libya a Study in Political Development. Baltimore: Johns Hopkins Press, 1963.

Kingdom of Libya, Ministry of Economy and Trade, Census and Statistical Department. General Population Census, 1964. Tripoli, n.d.

_____. Ministry of National Economy, Census and Statistical Department. Statistical Abstract 1964. Tripoli, 1964.

_____. Ministry of Planning and Development, Census and Statistical Department. Statistical Abstract 1967. Tripoli, 1968.

_____. Al-Ta'lim al-Dini fi Libya. Tripoli: Wizarat al-I'lam, 1966.

Knapp, Wilfrid. North West Africa: a Political and Economic Survey. 3d ed. Oxford: Oxford University Press, 1977.

"Law No. 176 of the year 1392 AH, 1972 AD." Official Gazette 10 (December 23, 1972): 3076-77.

Le Tourneau, R. L. "Libyan Education and its Development." UNESCO, Report of the Mission to Libya. Frankfurt: Johannes Weisbecker, 1952.

Libyan Arab Republic (LAR), Council for Rural Development. Ma' Masira al-Tanmiya al-Zira'iya al-Mutakamila. Tripoli, 1976.

_____. Ma'q Munjazat Mashru' Wadi al-Raml al-Qarbulli. Tripoli, n.d.

143

_____. General Women's Association. Al-Mar'a fi al-Tashri'at al-Arabiya al-Libiya. n.p., n.d.

_____. Maslahat al-Ihsa' wal-Ta'dad. Al-Nata'ij al-Awaliya lil-Ta'dad al-Zira'i, 1974. Tripoli: al-'Asriya Press, 1974.

_____. Ministry of Culture and Education. Taqrir 'an A'mal Wizarat al-Ta'lim wal-Tarbiya wa Aham Injazatiha fi al-Sanawat ma ba'd al-Thawra. Tripoli, 1974.

_____. Taqrir 'an Qita' al-Ta'lim wal-Tarbiya min 68/69 ila 1975. Pamphlet. n.p., n.d.

_____. Ministry of Culture and Education, Department of Planning and Development. Ihsa'at al-Ta'lim fi al-Jumhuriya al-'Arabiya al-Libiya 'an al-'Am al-Dirasi 1394-1395 AH, 1974-1975 AD. Tripoli: Government Press, n.d.

_____. Ministry of Culture and Education, Directorate of Planning. Dirasa Tarikhiya 'an Tatawwur al-Ta'lim fi al-Jumhuriya al-'Arabiya al-Libiya min 'Ahd al-'Uthmani ila Waqtina 1394 AH, 1974 AD. n.p., n.d.

_____. Ministry of Health. Al-Khadamat al-Sihhiya fi Saba' Sanawat 1389-1396 AH, 1969-1976 AD. Tripoli, n.d.

_____. Ministry of Planning. "Taqrir 'an Wadi' al Qiwa al-'Amila." Mimeographed. 1974.

_____. Ministry of Planning, Census and Statistics Department. Al-Dalil al-Jughrafi, Muhafadhat Tarablus. Tripoli: Al-Matba'a al-Libiya, 1973.

_____. Al-Ihsa'at al-Hayawiya 1392 AH, 1972 AD. Tripoli, n.d.

_____. Al-Majmu'a al-Ihsa'iya 1391 AH, 1971 AD. Tripoli, 1973.

_____. Ministry of Planning and Scientific Research. Al-Majmu'a al-Ihsa'iya 1393 AH, 1973 AD. Tripoli: Government Press, 1975.

_____. Ministry of Planning and Scientific Research, Census and Statistics Department. Al-Majmu'a al-Ihsa'iya 1394 AH, 1974 AD. Tripoli, 1976.

_____. Ministry of Planning and Scientific Research, Economic and

Social Planning Division. Report on Economic Growth During the Period 1971-1974. Tripoli, 1975.

____. Ministry for Social Affairs and Social Security. Dalil al-Ihsa'at al-Ijtima'iya 1395 AH, 1975 AD. Vol. 1. Tripoli, n.d.

____. Munjazat Wizarat al-Shu'un al-Ijtima'iya wal-Daman al-Ijtima'i 1396AH, 1976 AD. Tripoli, n.d.

____. Secretariat of Planning. Al-Ihsa'at al-Hayawiya 1393 AH, 1973 AD. Tripoli, n.d.

Libyan University, The. Dalil al-Jami'a al-Libiya 1971-1972. n.p., 1972.

Mansur, 'Ali 'Ali. Khutwa Ra'ida Nahwa Tatbiq Ahkam al-Shari'a al-Islamiya fi al-Jumhuriya al-'Arabiya al-Libiya. Beirut: Dar al-Fatwa, 1972.

Mayer, Ann. "Development in the Law of Marriage and Divorce in Libya since the 1969 Revolution." Journal of African Law 22 (Spring 1978): 30-42.

Naji, Mahmud. Kitab Tarablus al-Gharb. Translated from the Turkish to Arabic by 'Abd al-Salam Adham and Muhammad al-Usta. Beirut: Matba'a al-Ghurayib, n.d.

Nelson, Harold D., ed. Libya a Country Study. 3d ed. Washington, D.C.: Government Printing Office for Foreign Areas Studies, The American University, 1979.

al-Nimri, Michel. "Libya fi 'Asr al-Jamahir, al-Lijan al-Thawriya, Itar al-Thawra al-Siyasiya." Al-Safir, August 19, 1980, p. 11.

Paulston, Rolland G. Society, Schools and Progress in Peru. New York: Pergamon Press, 1971.

al-Qadhdhafi, Mu'ammar. Al-Kitab al-Akhdar, al-Fasl al-Awal, Hal Mushkilat al-Dimuqratiya, Sultat al-Sha'b. n.p., n.d. [1976?].

____. Al-Kitab al-Akhdar, al-Fasl al-Thani, Hal al-Mashkal al-Iqtisadi, al-Ishtirakiya. Tripoli: al-Sharikat al-'Amma lil-Nashr wal-Tawzi' wal-I'lan, 1977.

____. Min Ahadith al-'Aqid Mu'ammar al-Qadhdhafi fi al-Sahafa al-

'Arabiya wal-'Alamiya from August 2, 1973 to April 29, 1974. Tripoli: al-Thawra al-'Arabiya, n.d.

_____. Al-Sijil al-Qawmi, Bayanat, wa Khutab, wa Ahadith 1970-1971. Vol. 2. n.p., n.d.

_____. Al-Sijil al-Qawmi, Bayanat, wa Khutab, wa Ahadith 1971-1972. Vol. 3. Tripoli: al-Thawra al-'Arabiya, n.d.

_____. Al-Sijil al-Qawmi, Bayanat, wa Khutab, wa Ahadith 1972-1973. Vol. 4. Tripoli: al-Thawra al-'Arabiya, n.d.

_____. Al-Sijil al-Qawmi, Bayanat, wa Khutab, wa Ahadith 1973-1974. Vol. 5. Tripoli, n.d.

_____. Al-Sijil al-Qawmi, Bayanat, wa Khutab, wa Ahadith 1974-1975. Vol. 6. Tripoli: al-Thawra al-'Arabiya, n.d.

_____. Al-Sijil al-Qawmi, Bayanat, wa Khutab, wa Ahadith 1975-1976. Vol. 7. Tripoli: al-Thawra al-'Arabiya, n.d.

_____. Al-Sijil al-Qawmi, Bayanat, wa Khutab, wa Ahadith 1976-1977. Vol. 8. Tripoli, n.d.

"Qarar bi I'adat al-Tijara." Al-Zahf al-Akhdar 8 (August 4, 1980): 1-2.

al-Shaykh, Rif'at Ghanami. Tatawwur al-Ta'lim fi Libya fi al-'Usur al-Haditha. Benghazi: Dar al-Tanmiya lil-Nashr wal-Tawzi', 1972.

al-Sharkasi, Muhammad Mustafa. Lamhat 'An al-Awda' al-Iqtisadiya fi Libya Athna' al-'Ahd al-Itali. Tunis: al-'Arabiya lil-Kitab, 1976.

Shukri, Muhammad Fu'ad. Al-Sanusiya Din wa Dawla. Cairo: Dar al-Fikr al-'Arabi, 1948.

Socialist People's Libyan Arab Jamahiriya (SPLAJ), Council for Reclamation of Land, Executive Committee for Sahl al-Jafara. Al-Mar'a wal-Thawra al-Zira'iya fi al-Rif. Tripoli: Matba'at al-Rif, 1977.

_____. Department of Information and Cultural Affairs. Facts and Figures. Tripoli, 1977.

_____. Secretariat of Agriculture. Munjazat al-Thawra al-Zira'iya fi Majal al-Zira'a. Vol. 4. Tripoli, n.d.

_____. Secretariat for Culture and Education, Center for Educational Research and Documentation. Tashri'at al-Ta'lim fi al-Jamahiriya al-'Arabiya al-Libiya al-Sha'biya Ishtirakiya 1389-1394 AH, 1969-1974 AD. Tripoli, 1977.

_____. Secretariat of Education and Culture, Center for Documentation and Research. "Al-Tawthiq wal-Buhuth al-Tarbawiya." Mimeographed. n.p., n.d.

_____. Secretariat of the Interior, General Directorate for Security Affairs, Center for Research in Criminology. Taqrir 'an Halat al-Jarima 1396 AH, 1976 AD. Tripoli, n.d.

_____. Secretariat of Planning. Al-Ihsa'at al-Hayawiya 1394 AH, 1974 AD. Tripoli, n.d.

_____. Al-Ihsa'at al-Hayawiya 1396 AH, 1976 AD. Tripoli, n.d. [1978?].

_____. Secretariat of Planning, Census and Statistics Department. Nata'ij al-Ta'dad al-'Am lil-Sukkan, 1393 AH, 1973 AD, Benghazi. Tripoli: Government Press, 1977.

_____. Nata'ij al-Ta'dad al-'Am lil-Sukkan, 1393 AH, 1973 AD, Darna. Tripoli: Government Press, 1977.

_____. Nata'ij al-Ta'dad al-'Am lil-Sukkan, 1393 AH, 1973 AD, Gharyan. Tripoli: Government Press, 1977.

_____. Nata'ij al-Ta'dad al-'Am lil Sukkan, 1393 AH, 1973 AD, Al-Jabal al-Akhdar. Tripoli: Government Press, 1977.

_____. Nata'ij al-Ta'dad al-'Am lil-Sukkan, 1393 AH, 1973 AD, Al-Khalij. Tripoli: Government Press, 1977.

_____. Nata'ij al-Ta'dad al-'Am lil-Sukkan, 1393 AH, 1973 AD, Khums. Tripoli: Government Press, 1977.

_____. Nata'ij al-Ta'dad al-'Am lil-Sukkan, 1393 AH, 1973 AD, Masrata. Tripoli: Government Press, 1977.

_____. Nata'ij al-Ta'dad al-'Am lil-Sukkan, 1393 AH, 1973 AD, Sabha. Tripoli: Government Press, 1977.

____. Nata'ij al-Ta'dad al-'Am lil-Sukkan, 1393 AH, 1973 AD, Tripoli. Tripoli: Government Press, 1977.

____. Nata'ij al-Ta'dad al-'Am lil-Sukkan, 1393 AH, 1973 AD, Al-Zawiya. Tripoli: Government Press, 1977.

____. Population Census Summary Data 1393 AH, 1973 AD. Tripoli: Government Press, 1977.

____. Secretariat for Social Affairs and Social Security. Al-Kitab al-Sanawi li-Munjazat 1397 AH, 1977 AD. Tripoli: n.d.

SPLAJ, Secretariat for Social Affairs and Social Security. Dalil al-Ihsa' at al-Ijtima'uja 1395 AH, 1975 AD. Vol. 3. Tripoli, n.d.

Souriau, Christiane. "La Société Féminine en Libye." Revue de L'Occident Musulman et de la Méditérranée 16 (1èr et 2em trimestre, 1969).

Steele-Greig, A. J. History of Education in Tripolitania. Tripolitania: Government Press, 1948.

____. A Short History of Education in Tripolitania. Tripolitania: Department of Education, 1947.

Tarablus al-Gharb, Ghurfat al-Tijara wal-Sina'a. Al-Dalil al-Tijari 1968-1969. Beirut: al-Ghuraiyib Press, 1969.

Thawrat al-Sha'b al-'Arabi al-Libi. Vol. 1. Benghazi, 1972.

University of Benghazi, Research Center. Lamha 'an al-Wadi' al-Iqtisadi wal-Ijtima'i lil-Mar'a fi al-Jumhuriya al-'Arabiya al-Libiya. Benghazi, 1975.

U.S., Department of Commerce. Office of Technical Services. Joint Publications Research Service (JPRS). Translations on Near East and North Africa. "Citizens Urged to Buy their Goods from People's Markets," from al-Muntijun, July 7, 1979. JPRS 74217, pp. 40-41.

____. "Future Markets Without Traders," from al-Usbu' al-Siyasi, January 1, 1979. JPRS 72901, pp. 131-34.

____. "Interview with Director General of Economy Secretariat, Fawzi al-Shakshuki," from al-Usbu' al-Siyasi, August 10, 1979. JPRS 74377, pp. 34-37.

_____. "Law on Property Ownership Published." Tripoli, Domestic Services, May 6, 1978. JPRS 71325, pp. 80-82.

_____. Musa al-Ashkham, "The Religious Principles of the Ideology of al-Jamahiriya," from al-Usbu' al-Siyasi, March 2, 1979. JPRS 73322, pp. 90-94.

_____. "Role of Tribalism in al-Jamahiriyah Reviewed," from al-Usbu' al-Siyasi, March 2, 1979. JPRS 73322, pp. 84-89.

_____. Sayyid al-Jabarti, "A Little Dictator in Our Home," from al-Usbu' al-Thaqafi, January 19, 1979. JPRS 74217, pp. 40-41.

_____. "Tuesday Market: Juha's Secret-Filled House: Hundreds of Producers in Grip of Middlemen and Wholesalers," from al-Usbu' al-Siyasi, August 3, 1979. JPRS 74316, pp. 96-101.

_____. "Workers Take over Private Sector Companies," from al-Usbu' al-Siyasi, September 4, 1978. JPRS 72039, pp. 62-64.

Voll, John. "The Sudanese Mahdi: Frontier Fundamentalist." International Journal of Middle East Studies 10 (May 1979): 145-66.

World Health Organization. World Health Statistics. Vol. 1. Geneva, 1977.

al-Zantani, 'Abd al-Wahhab Muhammad. La Watha'iq October bal Watha'iq al-Wahda. Benghazi, n.d.

PERIODICALS

Arab Report and Record. London, 1968-78.

Al-Fajr al-Jadid. Tripoli, 1977-78.

Al-Fallah. Tripoli, 1975-78.

Jamahiriya Review. London, 1980-.

Al-Mar'a. Tripoli, 1976-.

Al-Mustaqbal. Paris, 1977-.

Nisa'al-Jamahiriya. Tripoli, 1978-.

Al-Safir. Beirut, 1974-.

Al-Zahf al-Akhdar. Tripoli, 1980-.

INDEX

Libya, prerevolution socioeconomic structure of, 109-
13; dominant role of foreigners, 111-12; growth of public
sector over private, 112-13;
segmentation and fragmen-
tation, 109-10, [Misrata an
example, 110-11]
Libyan University, 40
Libyan-Egyptian border war (July
1977), 135, 137, 138
lijan thawriya (revolutionary
committees), 121

Ma'ad Sabha, Institute of (al-
Jaghbub), 37
Ma'had Sabha al-Dini, Institute
of (Sabha), 37
mahallas (administrative divi-
sions), 1
al-Mahdi, Sayyid, 94, 95
Mahdiya movement (Sudan), 93
mahr (male dowry), 57-58
Majlis al-Ikhwan, 19
Malik ibn Ans, Institute of (al-
Bayda), 37; (Tripoli), 37
Malikite school of jurisprudence,
94, 99, 100
Mansur, 'Ali 'Ali, 99
al-Mar'a (magazine), 63
Maslata, 59, 63
Masrata, 5
Misrata, 39, 43-44, 67, 77,
110-11, 112, 114
Muhammad, Prophet, 100, 101,
102, 104
Murad Pasha, Institute of, 18
Muslim Brothers, 94

Najd, 93
National Congress, 111
nomads and seminomads, 11-14,
117-18
al-Numairi, Ja'far, 129, 131,
132

October War of 1973, 127, 128,
132, 133, 134

Palestine Liberation Organization
(PLO), 127, 128, 135, 136
Palestinian guerrillas, 127, 128,
129, 132
Palestinian Resistance Movement
(PRM), 129, 130, 132, 136
Pellet, Dr. Peter L., 56
POLISARIO, 136
Popular Democratic Front for the
Liberation of Palestine
(PDFLP), 132
Popular Front for the Liberation
of Palestine (PFLP), 132, 134
Popular Front for the Liberation
of Palestine-General Command
(PFLP-GC), 132
Population Census Summary, 13;
(1973), 53, 72
prostitution, 84-85
Public Agricultural Production
and Marketing Company, 119

qaba il (tribes), 1
Qabus, Sultan, 136
al-Qadhdhafi, Mu'ammar, 62, 64,
98-105 passim, 109, 126-138
passim; Arab Communists, cooperation with, 103; egalitarian
society, aim of, 114, 116,
[Marxist influence, 114-15];
Green Book of, 103, 113;
Islam, concept of, 98, 100,
101-105; natural socialism,
conception of, 113-14, 118,
[equality, 113-14]; political
ideas, 120-22, [a changed
society, 121; lijan thawriya,
121; parliamentary democracy,
criticism of, 120; radicaliza-
tion of his ideologies, 122;
unionism, fostering of, 120-21];
socioeconomic policies, 115-19,

154

[nomads and seminomads, 117–18; on nonproductive exploitation, 118–19; property ownership, 116–17; takeover of larger enterprises, 115–16]; Third Theory of, 103

Qar Yunis University, 40, 41, 47 (see also Benghazi, University of)

Qaramanlis, 19, 20

al-Qarbulli, 1, 5, 11, 78

Qarqarish, 2

Qasf Ahmad, 110

Qasr bin Ghashir, 1, 4, 11; sectors of, 1

al-Quwayri al-Dini, Institute of (Masarata), 37

Rabat Arab Summit (December 1969), 130–31

Rabi', Muhammad, 73

Ra's Jabir, 132

Ras 'Ubayda, Institute of (Benghazi), 37

rehabilitation centers for women, 83–86

Religious Institute of Gharyan, 37

Riyad Arab summit, 135, 138

Rogers Plan, 130

Revolutionary Council, 99

Sa'adah, Antun, 104

Sa'adi tribes, 111

Sabha, 5, 46, 97, 114

Sabri, 'Ali, 131

al-Sadat, Anwar, 128, 131–38 passim

al-Safir, 104

Sahl al-Jafara, 79

Sanusi, Sayyid Muhammad Ali, 19, 94–95, 97

Sanusi(ya) movement (Libya), 19–20, 93, 94, 98, 111; concept of basis of Islam, 99–100;

decline of, 98; emphasis on transcendence of God, 100–101; first stage, 94–95; Ikhwan, 96; Khaldunian symbiosis, 95; second stage, 95–96; third stage, 96–97

al-Sayyid Muhammid bin 'Ali al-Sanusi, Institute of (al-Bayda), 97

Second Sinai Agreement, 128

shari'a (canon law of Islam), 99–100, 102, 105, 132; courts, 96–97; law, 83

al-Sharif, Ahmad, 95

Shi'ite jurisprudence, schools of, 100

Sidi 'Abd al-Salam al-Asmar, Institute of (Zlitin), 97

Sirtica, 95, 98

Souriau, Christiane, 55, 59

Steadfastness and Confrontation Front (SCF), 128, 136–37

Steele-Greig, A. J., 21, 25, 26

Sudanese Communist Party, 132

Sunni jurisprudence, schools of, 99, 100

Sunni Muslims, 93

Suq al-Jum'a, 27

al-Suwani, 4

Tajura, 1, 4, 11, 18, 103

Third Theory (of al-Qadhdhafi), 103

Tripoli (municipality, city), 1, 5, 11, 18; major suburbs, 2–4; population, 5; schools in, 27; sectors of, 1

Tripoli, University of, 31, 39, 40, 41–42, 44, 75 (see also Al-Fateh University)

Tripoli Pact, 131

Tripoli Teachers' Training Center, 28

Tripolitania, 26, 96, 98, 109, 110, 112, 113, 127

Tubruq, 46
Tubruq-Benghazi Declaration, 131

'Umar ibn al-Khattab, Institute of (al-Zawiya), 37
UNESCO, 26
United Arab Republic, 131
United Nations, 134; Resolution 242, 127, 133, 134
urban areas, 10-11

Vital Statistics Bulletin for 1974, 53
Voice of the Arabs, 98

Wahhabi movement, 93, 94, 95
women in Libya: and crime, 80-86, [rehabilitation, 83-86; unreported crimes, 80-82]; and divorce, 63-64; education, 73-80; fewer than men, 53-56; illiteracy of, 26, 27-28, 31, 43-44, 48, 52-53, 78, 80; and marriage, 56-57, [ceremony and festivities, 60-61; choice of partner, 58-60 58-60; laws on, 62; mahr (male dowry), 57-58; other

payments, 58; polygyny, 61-62]; traditional position, 52-53; working, in rural areas, 70-73; working, in urban sector, 64-70, [at-home work, 67, 68; clerical and administrative, 66; house-keeping services, 67, 68; industrial, 66-67; laws concerning, 68-69; nursing and health services, 65, 68; pension and compensations, 70; teachers, 65]
Women Organization of Benghazi, 83
Women's Union, 66
World Health Organization, 55

al-Zahf al-Akhdar, 121
Zawia, 39
al-Zawiya, 5, 7, 27, 71, 97
zawiyas, 18-19, 94, 96, 97, 101
Zayd bin Thabit, Institute of (al-Khalij), 37, 39
Zleiten, 39
Zlitin, 97
Zuwara, 103

ABOUT THE AUTHORS

MARIUS K. DEEB teaches cultural history and Middle Eastern politics at the American University of Beirut. He previously taught at Indiana University, Bloomington, and chaired the Middle East Program at Kent State University. He has been a Senior Associate Member at St. Antony's College, Oxford University, a Visiting Senior Fellow at Princeton University, and a Visiting Scholar at Georgetown

Dr. Deeb has published widely in the area of Middle Eastern politics and history. His articles have appeared in the International Journal of Middle Eastern Studies, Middle Eastern Studies, and the Canadian Review of Studies in Nationalism. He is the author of Party Politics in Egypt: The Wafd and its Rivals 1919-1939, St. Antony's Middle East Monographs Series, No. 9, London, 1979; and The Lebanese Civil War, Praeger Publishers, New York, 1980.

Dr. Deeb holds a B.A. and an M.A. from the American University of Beirut, Lebanon, and a Ph.D. from Oxford University, Oxford, England.

MARY JANE DEEB is at present teaching sociology at Haigazian University, in Beirut. She received her B.A. and M.A. degrees from the American University in Cairo, where she was also University Fellow. She has been a Research Associate for the Ford Foundation in Beirut, and a Research Associate at the Arab Development Institute in Tripoli, Libya. She was Consultant for the United Nations Economic Commission for Western Asia, and Consultant for the United Nations Children's Fund in Beirut. She has carried out several research projects for the institutions she has worked for, including studies on the social problems of narcotics in Lebanon, women, education, Basic Service Units, and social change in the Middle East. She is at present a Consultant for the Agency for International Development (AID).